CANAL HOUSE
COOKING

CANAL HOUSE
No. 6 Coryell Street
Lambertville, NJ 08530
thecanalhouse.com

ISBN 978-0-9827394-2-6

Printed in China

Book design by CANAL HOUSE, a group of artists who collaborate on design projects.
This book was designed by Melissa Hamilton, Christopher Hirsheimer & Teresa Hopkins.
Edited by Margo True & Copyedited by Valerie Saint-Rossy.
Editorial assistance by Julia Lee & Julie Sproesser
Photos credits
page 1: Andre Baranowski, page 6: Julia Lee

Distributed to the trade by
Andrews McMeel Publishing, LLC
an Andrews McMeel Universal company
1130 Walnut Street, Kansas City, Missouri 64106

www.andrewsmcmeel.com

11 12 13 14 OGP 10 9 8 7 6 5 4 3 2

ATTENTION: SCHOOLS AND BUSINESSES
Andrews McMeel books are available at quantity discounts with bulk purchase for
educational, business, or sales promotional use. For information, please e-mail
the Andrews McMeel Publishing Special Sales Department:
specialsales@amuniversal.com

CANAL HOUSE
COOKING

Volume N° 6

Hamilton & Hirsheimer

Welcome to Canal House—our studio, workshop, dining room, office, kitchen, and atelier devoted to good ideas and good work relating to the world of food. We write, photograph, design, and paint, but in our hearts we both think of ourselves as cooks first.

Our loft studio is in an old red brick warehouse. A beautiful lazy canal runs alongside the building. We have a simple galley kitchen. Two small apartment-size stoves sit snugly side by side against a white tiled wall. We have a dishwasher, but prefer to hand wash the dishes so we can look out of the tall window next to the sink and see the ducks swimming in the canal or watch the raindrops splashing into the water.

And every day we cook. Starting in the morning we tell each other what we made for dinner the night before. Midday, we stop our work, set the table simply with paper napkins, and have lunch. We cook seasonally because that's what makes sense. So it came naturally to write down what we cook. The recipes in our books are what we make for ourselves and our families all year long. If you cook your way through a few, you'll see that who we are comes right through in the pages: that we are crazy for tomatoes in summer, make braises and stews all fall, and turn oranges into marmalade in winter.

Canal House Cooking is home cooking by home cooks for home cooks. We use ingredients found in most markets. All the recipes are easy to prepare for the novice and experienced cook alike. We want to share them with you as fellow cooks along with our love of food and all its rituals. The everyday practice of simple cooking and the enjoyment of eating are two of the greatest pleasures in life.

CHRISTOPHER HIRSHEIMER served as food and design editor for *Metropolitan Home* magazine, and was one of the founders of *Saveur* magazine, where she was executive editor. She is a writer and a photographer.

MELISSA HAMILTON cofounded the restaurant Hamilton's Grill Room in Lambertville, New Jersey, where she served as executive chef. She worked at *Martha Stewart Living*, *Cook's Illustrated*, and at *Saveur* as the food editor.

Melissa and Christopher in the Canal House kitchen

The Best Grocery Store in the World
by Colman Andrews 7

It's Always Five O'Clock Somewhere

rhubarb syrup 12, amante 12, primavera 13, whiskey sour 13, greyhound 15
italian greyhound 15, salty dog 15, perro 15, perro salado 15

Crax & Butter For Dinner

pimiento cheese 18, blue cheese with black pepper 18
anchovy & lemon butter 18, smoked salmon butter 19, twirled-up goat cheese 19
tender cheese crackers 19, welsh rabbit 22, cheese & crackers 23
cheddar with mango chutney 23, canned sardines with sliced lemon 25
for anchovy lovers only 25, a can of tuna & some lemons 25

Soup's On

a rationale for making stocks & broths 28, beef broth 29
turkey broth 30, chicken broth 30, vegetable broth 31
meatless meatballs in broth 33, swiss chard & lemon soup 33
brothy beef short ribs 34, brothy beef short ribs & root vegetables 34
smoked fish stew 36, clam chowder 36, quick cioppino 37

Eat Your Vegetables

asparagus & company 40, blender lemon-butter sauce 40, favorite asparagus butter 40
asparagus frittata 40, asparagus risotto 41, broccoli rabe & chorizo 44
jansson's temptation 44, cauliflower with toasted spiced bread crumbs 45
in praise of escarole 48, braised escarole with white beans 49
escarole salad with lemon & parmesan 49, creamed spinach 52, spinach flan 52
steamed spinach 53, poached eggs 53, peas & potatoes 56
lillie's pasta with peas & ham 56, cutlets smothered in peas 57
mezzi rigatoni with peas & ricotta 57, "fresh" pea soup 58

succotash 59, baby limas with feta 59, favas & peas salad 61, fava mash 61
steamed rice 62, fried rice 63, notes on dried beans 66
basic cooked dried beans 67, lentils with roasted beets 67, black bean soup 69

OUT OF THE OCEAN AND INTO THE FRYING PAN
any night linguine with clam sauce 72, fried fish 73
tartar sauce 73, fish sticks 75, crab cakes 76

HOT CHICKS
canal house "rotisserie" chicken 80, gingered chicken in cream 81
chicken & rice 81, chicken cordon bleu 82
chicken kiev à la canal house 84, roasted chicken wings 85

THE MEAT OF THE MATTER
deluxe dinner of boiled meats 88, daube 90, stuffed cabbage 93
drunken sauerkraut with smoked pork chops 94, chopped steak marchand de vin 97

A CELEBRATION OF SPRING
stuffed spring eggs 100, stew of baby artichokes & favas 101
savory asparagus bread pudding 103, easter ham 104
meringues with strawberries & roasted rhubarb 105

SWEETIES
winter summer pudding 108, roasted orange marmalade toast 108
apricot compote 109, pound cake 110, apples tatin 111
boston cream pie 114, brownies 115, little chocolate turnovers 117

BREAKFAST ALL DAY LONG
neen's buttermilk love cakes 120, sour cream pancakes 121
the best waffles in the world 122, creamed chicken 123, eggs à la goldenrod 123

GETTING & GIVING

EARLY ON A SHOWERY SPRING MORNING, we meet for coffee at the shopping center midway between our houses. Then, revved up on caffeine, lists in hand, we each take a cart and head into ShopRite. The Canal House larder needs replenishing—we've been cooking like crazy—and besides, our cupboards at home are bare. We both need to get food for our own families.

We start out together, chatting away, rolling our carts side by side into the vegetable section. We see a bin filled with big fat local asparagus spears and we both stop and reach for the same bunch. Laughing, each of us steps back—no, you; no, you! Then we head off in different directions. Normally we're perimeter shoppers, sliding around the edges of the big store. We hit vegetables, hang a left, roll through meats, and hang another left at bread and dairy, then out the door we go. But today is different, we're not just racing through, checking items off the list. Actually, it's fun to be here on such a bustling Saturday morning. They're piping in "Good Vibrations", Muzak style, and a little grey-haired lady, groovin' to the tune, with hips swaying, stops and shuffles a dance move right there in the international food aisle. Then a voice interrupts the music. It's Archie Fagan, 82, the beloved store fixture who alerts shoppers that fresh, hot cinnamon buns are just out of the oven in the bakery department. "Come and get one to eat while you shop and buy a dozen to take home to the family, and stop by the deli department for some hot roast turkey and gravy, $5.99 a pound, for your dining pleasure." Archie could sell fleas to a dog, he's so smooth. He makes you smile and laugh, and you're glad you are there, hearing him go on.

We've both had love-hate relationships with supermarkets—pile it high and sell it low. We've been overwhelmed by the volume of product, but underwhelmed by the variety and quality. Most grocery stores have lost their human scale. They've turned into mega-supermarkets. In these warehouses of food, store clerks have little knowledge or affinity for the wares they sell. Signs tout ripe avocados that are hard as rocks, expensive fresh herbs that are anything but, and fish that can only be described as "fishy". Butchers unpack boxes of low-grade meats and stare at you blankly when you ask for their advice on how to cook a particular cut. The aisles are filling up with more and more anonymously (and badly) prepared foods. It's a sad state of affairs. We understand the need for convenience and ease, but to give up the vitality, flavor, and texture of food seems crazy.

ShopRite isn't a fancy store; everybody around here shops here. But it is a really good grocery store. It has great, helpful service, fair prices for quality goods, and the management brings in what shoppers want to buy. It's the place we rely on when the garden has gone to sleep and it's too cold for farmers' markets. When we venture up and down the aisles, we never fail to make new "friends"—a store-brand bottle of unfiltered Italian extra-virgin olive oil, cold-pressed from first-harvest olives for eight bucks a liter; bags of Meyer lemons; half-pound blocks of Kerrygold Irish butter; premium grade Nishiki medium-grain rice, $11.49 for a 5-pound bag. We think of this place as our own big pantry, stocked with cans of anchovies; tuna preserved in olive oil; cake, pastry, and all-purpose flours; peppercorns; and kosher salt. We choose organic when it makes sense and always support local products when we see them in the store. Fresh, wholesome food is the starting point of any recipe. And our good cooking relies on this good shopping.

We started a tradition three years ago—we shop for each other. We can't remember who started it, and it doesn't matter anyway. It began as an act of kindness for a busy friend. But as often happens, the giver gets a greater gift.

When we shop for each other, we step up the game, twirl it up a little. No boneless, skinless anythings. Into the cart go whole ducks and fat chickens. A breast of veal—she'll like the challenge. A ruffly savoy cabbage and some ground lamb: She'll figure out what to do with that. From the freezer section, a couple bags of frozen favas and peas, always good to have around. And cans of baby clams with a box of linguine. And, of course, the giver buys double of everything because she wants to cook all that good food, too. When we talk about it later—"So what did you make with that breast of veal?"—it turns out one of us uses the veal to enrich a broth and the other braises it with anchovies. One dismantles the chicken, roasting the wings, stuffing the breast with herbed butter Kiev style, while the other throws the whole bird right on the oven rack to cook over a big pan of root vegetables. We delight and surprise each other. Since so much heart and thought goes into these gifts, we both honor the effort by cooking well.

This expression of friendship helps us make friends with all our market has to offer. We don't shop for each other all the time, of course, but when we do, it sure takes the chore out of everyday shopping—for both of us.

Christopher & Melissa

Grocer Darrell Corti, "the professor", in the wine department of Corti Brothers

THE BEST GROCERY STORE IN THE WORLD
by
Colman Andrews

The big rectangular sign that sits high on a pole outside a low-slung work-aday-looking building on Freeport Boulevard in Sacramento reads "Corti Brothers Since 1947"; a smaller oval sign above it defines the place as a "Specialty Grocers". Inside, you will look in vain for frosted glass panels, trendy graphics, pin spots illuminating quotations from Brillat-Savarin, and other poncy modern food-shop furnishings. Instead, fluorescent lights shine down brightly on rows of standard shelving, neatly stocked; deli meats and cheese are stuck with old-style plastic price signs, the kind with numerals you can move around when something goes from $7.99 to $8.29 a pound. The smell in the air isn't freshly distressed pine flooring or the assistant manager's Acqua di Giò; it's food—the earthy aromas of meat and cheese, the woody perfume of coffee beans, the fragrances of sweet fruit and pungent garlic.

The important thing to remember about Corti Brothers is that while it may be a "specialty grocers", it is also a supermarket, in the traditional American sense. Fresh produce glistens in the kind of pristine abundance rarely found outside California. Fish and meat departments are well supplied, and feature everything you'd expect (boneless trout, salmon steaks, crab claws, mussels; T-bones and skirt steak, lamb chops, spareribs, chicken wings, and whole turkeys), albeit with a few surprises thrown in (stockfish as hard as a two-by-four, ground emu, corned beef tongue). You can order cold cuts sliced extra-thin here, pick up a couple of cans of beans, grab a head or two of iceberg, stock up on frozen orange juice and frozen ravioli. You can also buy skim milk, and toilet paper, and assorted victuals for Fluffy and Rex.

On the other hand, Corti Brothers would also be happy to send you home with a square-sided flask of Yanai Kanro Shoyu of Mitsuboshi soy sauce (unlike any you've ever imagined); or a bag of Ball Club Chippewa genuine wild rice; or a cake-like Loison panettone flavored with candied apricots and ginger; or a wedge of Montasio cheese from Latteria Perenzin in Italy's Julian Alps; or a bottle of Delamain 1982 Early Landed Cognac or of San Geminiano Aceto Balsamico Tradizionale Oro Riserva—at $499 for not quite three-and-a-half ounces, so you know we're not talking about the stuff they put in the salads over at the Olive Garden. Wines—hundreds of them, probably three-quarters of which the average wine lover has never heard of, to his or her detriment—stand shoulder to shoulder in glorious array here, as do phalanxes of olive oils. Italian bitters? Single-malt Scotch? Fresh mozzarella or aged prosciutto? Rare Chinese tea? Canned haggis? Corti Brothers has got you covered.

Corti Brothers, in other words, is an unassuming treasure-house of absolutely superb food and drink items that share space easily with a vast catalogue of more pedestrian things. It serves its community—every stratum of that community. A measure of how well it does that may be seen from the fact that when the market lost its lease a few years back and another kind of food shop (cue the frosted glass and the Brillat-Savarin) announced plans to take over the space, the public outcry was so loud and large that the newcomers backed off and Corti Brothers was able to renew its lease for ten more years.

Corti Brothers is run today not by a Corti brother, but by Darrell Corti, the son of one sibling (Frank) and thus the nephew of the other (Gino). Darrell is a medium-size, gray-haired gentleman of Genoese descent, with long ears, a proud chin, and a mien that seems both amiable and scholarly. When he's working, he usually sports a dark blue smock, like something a grocer might have worn a hundred years ago. And if you were to be so ingenuous as to ask Darrell what he does for a living, he would most likely respond, as if it were the most obvious thing in the world, that he is exactly that: a grocer.

And so he is, undeniably. But he is a grocer like Itzhak Perlman is a fiddler, or Kobe Bryant shoots some hoops. Darrell Corti is the not-so-secret secret of Corti Brothers—the reason it is unique, and commands such respect and loyalty. His father and uncle founded their business with the notion of not just selling food but talking to people about it, bringing it alive in ways that conventional supermarkets can't. Darrell took the idea and ran with it, first building up the wine department (which was his entry-level bailiwick within the store), then going off into the world to learn about and bring back pretty much the best of everything else and then share it with his customers. He learns about things because he is genuinely interested in them—though of course as a grocer, he also learns about them because the more he can evocatively describe the treasures he sells, the more his customers will buy them. "We don't have every good thing in the world here," he likes to say, "but everything we do have is very good."

Along the way, Darrell has accumulated a range of knowledge that is truly encyclopedic—which he shares freely and with obvious pleasure. When he was inducted into The Culinary Institute of America's Vintners Hall of Fame in 2008 (and he would be the first to tell you that while vintner is commonly used as a synonym for "winemaker", its original meaning was "wine merchant"), the proclamation, besides acknowledging his key role in helping to promote the California wine industry, noted that he "has mentored a generation of seminal food and wine professionals with impeccable taste and articulate discourse."

I don't remember the first time I met Darrell Corti, which is curious because Darrell is one of the more memorable fellows I have ever encountered. I suspect that it must have been sometime in the early to mid-1970s, though, and I do recall that the first time I referred to Darrell in print, I spelled his name "Daryl." I also once incurred his thankfully short-lived animus by calling him a know-it-all.

Well, hell, he *is* a know-it-all. But he's a know-it-all who really does—at least in regards to food and drink and the proper service and sybaritic enjoyment thereof. (Actually, he also has a pretty good knowledge of Romance languages both commonplace and marginal, European cultural history, opera, incense—about which he has occasionally threatened to write a book—and probably a few hundred other subjects.) His friends sometimes call him "the professor". When the winery sales manager Gretchen Allen-Wilcox launched a Facebook fan page devoted to Darrell—who, incidentally, would likely have had no idea what a Facebook fan page was at the time, and probably still doesn't quite grasp the concept or particularly want to—she dubbed it "Darrell Corti will always know more than you about Food and Wine". As she explained in an early post on the site, when she and her husband, who at one point had worked as a deli manager at Corti Brothers, "would occasionally find a subject that we had researched and with pride, we would present what we knew to Darrell. Inevitably, he would not only correct us on our misinformation, but proceed to provide a historical recount of the product, its country of origin, and its historical significance. Dejected but not defeated, we would retreat back to the books to try to find holes in his stories. We never could."

Well, of course not. I've long since learned that there's no percentage in trying to one-up Darrell. Even if it happens that you do somehow know something about food or wine that he doesn't, he'll likely understand the significance of what you know better than you do—and if your fragment of knowledge leads to something good, he'll figure out pretty quickly how that something can be incorporated into a well-seasoned life. And the next time you stop by Corti Brothers, you'll probably find it on the shelf.

Colman Andrews, our dear friend and mentor, was the cofounder of *Saveur* and is now editorial director of *thedailymeal.com*.

it's always five o'clock somewhere

RHUBARB SYRUP
makes 4 cups

One of the first edible plants up in the spring is mighty rhubarb, with its heart-shaped leaves and long succulent bright red or green stalks. Rhubarb is known and relied on for its purgative powers—it's a natural spring tonic. If you want to make this before the season, frozen rhubarb works just fine. Hugh Fearnley-Whittingstall turned us on to rhubarb syrup in his *The River Cottage Year* (Hodder & Stoughton, 2003).

4 pounds fresh rhubarb, cut into pieces, or 4 pounds frozen rhubarb
1⅓ cups superfine sugar

2 cups (10 blood oranges) fresh blood orange or orange juice

Put the rhubarb and sugar into a pot and bring to a boil over medium heat. Reduce the heat to low and simmer for 50 minutes. Add the orange juice and cook for 10 minutes. Use a fine sieve to strain the juice into a bowl. Return the juice to the pot, bring to a gentle boil, and cook for about 20 minutes, until it has reduced to a light syrup. Measure the syrup and, if necessary, continue to cook over medium heat until it reduces to about 4 cups. Store in a covered container in the refrigerator for up to 1 month.

AMANTE

This drink borrows elements from two great classics: a sugary rim from the sidecar and tequila from the margarita. Deliciously tart rhubarb and sweet orange juice stand in for limes. We prepare our glasses ahead of time, first by wetting the rim with a little rhubarb syrup or orange juice, then rolling the edge of each glass in superfine sugar. We stash the glasses in the freezer for a while so they get frosty. They won't stay that way for very long once you take them out, but they look so beautiful and appealing while they do.

For each drink we mix together 3 ounces Rhubarb Syrup, and 2 ounces tequila, then pour it into sugar-rimmed glasses filled with lots of ice. We garnish the drink with a slice of orange. Or if you prefer your drink "up", sugar the rim of a stemmed glass and put it in the freezer until it is frosty, then pour in the cocktail.——*makes 1*

PRIMAVERA

Spring, with all its glories—its lightness, its frothiness—deserves to have a drink created in its honor. Normally we don't like to mess with, or muck up wine—how can you improve on a vintner's miracle? But in the spirit of the season we add (give or take) 2 ounces Rhubarb Syrup (page 12) to a Champagne flute, then pour in about 4 ounces ice-cold Prosecco. Spring has sprung! ——*makes 1*

For a nonalcoholic drink, pour 3 ounces Rhubarb Syrup into a stemmed glass. Add cold bubbly water. Serve over ice, if you like. ——*makes 1*

WHISKEY SOUR
makes 2

Early bartending guides mention this classic, whiskey made tart with lemon juice, sweet with sugar, and sometimes frothy with egg white or seltzer, but the classic recipe is rarely what bartenders follow these days. Bastardized over the years with bottled and powdered sour mixes, it is overly sweet and tangy—a shame when the real thing is so simple to make.

Our version is simpler still. We forgo the egg white and mix our citrus juices, focusing on freshness rather than texture. Instead of the classic garnish of an orange slice and a maraschino cherry, we opt for a slice of lemon to match what's in the glass.

3 ounces whiskey or bourbon whiskey
1½ ounces fresh lemon juice
1½ ounces fresh lime juice

1 ounce Simple Syrup, below, or
2 tablespoons superfine sugar
2 thin lemon slices

Put the whiskey, lemon juice, lime juice, and simple syrup, into an ice cube–filled cocktail shaker, cover, and shake vigorously. Divide the cocktail between 2 rocks glasses, adding a few more ice cubes to each. Garnish with lemon.

SIMPLE SYRUP ❦ Put 1 cup superfine sugar and ½ cup water in a heavy-bottomed saucepan. Cook over medium-low heat, gently swirling the pan to help dissolve the sugar as it melts. When the sugar comes to a boil, cover, and cook for about 1 minute. Let the syrup cool to room temperature. Store in the refrigerator for up to 6 months.

When the canal alongside our studio is frozen hard, it's easy to forget that other parts of the country are bathed in sunny fruit-ripening warmth. Cutting into a juicy grapefruit with its burst of fresh citrus scent transports us there. Grapefruit—from California, Texas, and Florida—are in their prime from January to April and we are so glad to see them piled high at our grocery store. The sweeter Ruby Reds from Texas are our favorites to juice for cocktails, so we buy them by the bagful while they are plentiful.

GREYHOUND

Before vodka became so fashionable, many cocktails like these were originally made with gin. We like our dogs either way.

Fill two small glasses with ice. To each add 2 ounces gin or vodka and 4 ounces fresh pink or Ruby Red grapefruit juice. Give each a gentle stir. ——*makes 2*

ITALIAN GREYHOUND ❧ Follow the directions for the Greyhound, adding a splash of Campari to each cocktail.

SALTY DOG ❧ Follow the directions for the Greyhound but first moisten the rim of each glass with grapefruit juice, then roll the rim in a saucer of kosher salt.

PERRO ❧ Follow the directions for the Greyhound, substituting 100 percent agave blanco tequila for the gin or vodka and adding the juice of ½ a fat, smooth-skinned lime to each cocktail.

PERRO SALADO ❧ Follow the directions for the Perro but first moisten the rim of each glass with the cut side of 1 lime wedge then roll the rim in a saucer of kosher salt.

crax & butter for dinner

PIMIENTO CHEESE
makes 2 cups

We spread this Southern classic on Club Crackers instead of eating it the other traditional way—between two slices of soft white bread.

8 ounces extra sharp Cheddar, finely grated

One 4-ounce jar pimientos, drained and chopped

1 teaspoon grated yellow onion

½ cup mayonnaise

⅓ cup cream cheese

½ teaspoon salt

¼ teaspoon pepper

Pinch of ground cayenne

Put the Cheddar, pimientos, onions, mayonnaise, cream cheese, salt, pepper, and cayenne in a medium bowl and mix with a wooden spoon until it is well blended and the Cheddar becomes creamy. Refrigerate for about 1 hour before serving. It will keep in the refrigerator for up to 1 week.

BLUE CHEESE WITH BLACK PEPPER

This savory butter is great on grilled steaks, lamb chops, roast chicken, and baked potatoes—oh yeah, and crackers too.

Put 8 ounces (2 sticks) softened butter (preferably Irish) into a bowl or the bowl of a food processor. Add 4 ounces good blue cheese and lots of freshly ground black pepper too. Use a fork to blend it together into a coarse mash or blend it together in the food processor for a smoother butter. —— *makes about 1½ cups*

ANCHOVY & LEMON BUTTER

Each little smear of this salty citrus spread packs a whole lot of flavor. On a cracker, it is the perfect cocktail crunch as you sip an aperitif.

Put 8 ounces (2 sticks) softened unsalted butter (preferably Irish) into a bowl or the bowl of a food processor. Add 12 oil-packed anchovy filets, ⅛ teaspoon ground cayenne, and the grated zest of 1 lemon. Use a fork to blend it together by hand into a coarse mash or blend it together in the food processor for a smoother butter. —— *makes 1 cup*

SMOKED SALMON BUTTER

Use the best hot- or cold-smoked salmon available. If you don't have preserved lemon, use the grated rind of a fresh lemon and a good squeeze of its juice. Put 8 ounces (2 sticks) softened unsalted butter (preferably Irish) into a bowl or the bowl of a food processor. Add 4 ounces smoked salmon, ⅛ teaspoon ground cayenne, and the rind of 1 small preserved lemon minus the pith. Use a fork to blend it together by hand into a coarse mash or blend it together in the food processor for a smoother butter. —— *makes about 1½ cups*

TWIRLED-UP GOAT CHEESE

This is hardly a recipe, rather it's more of a reminder. We buy fresh creamy goat cheese made regionally, available nationally, at our grocery store. It lacks the great provenance and earthy tang of an artisanal chevre, so we feel free to dress up its mild flavor. Sometimes we spice up a 5-ounce pyramid of chevre with freshly cracked black pepper, really good extra-virgin olive oil (sometimes lemon-flavored), and minced fresh chives. Or we'll spoon the chevre onto a small plate, give it a good drizzle of really good extra-virgin olive oil, then generously sprinkle on Fennel Spice Mix (page 45). —— *makes a generous ½ cup*

TENDER CHEESE CRACKERS

These tender, buttery crackers are to their store-bought cousins what the linen cocktail napkin is to its paper counterpart. Bet you can't eat just one! Cut about 6 ounces parmigiano-reggiano into small chunks and put them into the bowl of a food processor fitted with a steel blade. Process until the cheese is finely ground. Add 1 cup flour, ½ teaspoon each of salt and pepper, and a pinch of ground cayenne and pulse a few times. With the processor running, add 4 tablespoons unsalted butter a tablespoon at a time. Then dribble in up to 5 tablespoons ice water and process until the dough comes together in a ball. Flatten the dough into a disc, wrap in wax paper, and refrigerate for at least 1 hour or up to a day. Roll out the dough between 2 pieces of wax paper to a thickness of ⅛ inch, cut into little circles or squares, and bake in a preheated 350° oven until puffed and golden, 7–10 minutes. —— *serves 8*

Overleaf: clockwise from upper left, Twirled-Up Goat Cheese, Tender Cheese Crackers, Pimiento Cheese, Anchovy & Lemon Butter, Smoked Salmon Butter, Blue Cheese with Black Pepper

WELSH RABBIT

My little brother Ian and I shared so much growing up. The youngest of five, we were often paired together. When I was eleven I decided to teach myself to cook. Ian was my taster. My first effort, roasted leg of veal massaged for 30 minutes with olive oil, then slathered in Dijon mustard, s & p, and chopped fresh rosemary, was a great success. Baked Alaska, not such a great success. One dreary spring we made a fort in a big closet under the back stairs. We piled in blankets and pillows and read *Jane Eyre* to each other using a flashlight to illuminate the pages. I'd slip out of the closet into the kitchen and make what I thought was Welsh rabbit—thick slices of sharp Cheddar laid on top of Ryvita crackers and sprinkled with chili powder, then grilled under the broiler. I'd serve these exotic treats with a blender whirl-up of hot milk with instant coffee, sweetened with lots of sugar. We would sip the foamy brew and crunch into the spicy melted cheese crackers as we read Charlotte Brontë's dramatic tale.

Real Welsh rabbit is a dish of melted Cheddar on toast that has never seen hide nor "hare" of a rabbit! The origin of the name has lots of lore. It could have been named, tongue in cheek, for a dish served when the hunter returned home empty-handed, or because cheese was the poor man's meat. Leeks, one of the national symbols of Wales, seems like a natural and tasty addition. —— CH

Wash, trim, and slice 2 large leeks. Melt 2 tablespoons butter in a pan over medium heat. Sauté the leeks until soft but not browned, 15 minutes. Set aside.

Melt 2 tablespoons butter in a heavy medium pot over low heat. Sprinkle in 2 tablespoons flour and salt and pepper to taste and cook, stirring with a wooden spoon, for about 3 minutes. This cooks the "raw" flavor out of the flour; take care not to let it brown. Add 1 tablespoon English or Dijon mustard, a splash of Worcestershire sauce, and a pinch of black pepper. Gradually whisk in 1 cup good pale ale, then stir 5 ounces grated Cheddar into the sauce.

Preheat the broiler. Divide the leeks between 6 slices toasted bread. Spoon the melted cheese over the leeks. Broil until lightly browned on top. You can also spoon the leeks and cheese into split baked potatoes. —— *serves 4–6*

CHEESE & CRACKERS

McSorley's Old Ale House, the quintessential Irish workingman's pub in New York City's East Village, is famous (or infamous, depending on your point of view) for many things, including its ale, its sawdust-covered floors, its exclusion of women until 1970, and its current popularity with college kids. But in my family, its reputation has everything to do with the cheese and crackers platter they serve with their beer—Cheddar, saltines, spicy mustard, and sliced raw onions. My father, who taught scenic and lighting design in the seventies at nearby New York University, would often grab a beer there with his friends before heading back home to his family. The platter had a rustic, casual quality he loved and ever since then, that's how we put out cheese and crackers. ——MH

Put ½ wheel good sharp Cheddar on a large board with an opened sleeve of saltine crackers, a sliced, peeled yellow onion, and an open jar of spicy mustard (we like to use Dijon) next to it. Everyone can make their own cracker with a piece of cheese, a smear of mustard, and a piece of onion on top. Bottoms up! ——*serves a crowd*

CHEDDAR WITH MANGO CHUTNEY

When we have a good pullman loaf and Cheddar on hand, we'll make ourselves a modified version of the British ploughman's lunch, adding a little mango chutney instead of the traditional Branston Pickle between the slices. But when we need a snack to go with our tippling, we put a thick slice of good sharp aged Cheddar on a thin wheat cracker (we're partial to Stoned Wheat Thins, though the name does make us chortle a little!) and add a small spoonful of Major Grey's mango chutney on top. ——*make as many as you want*

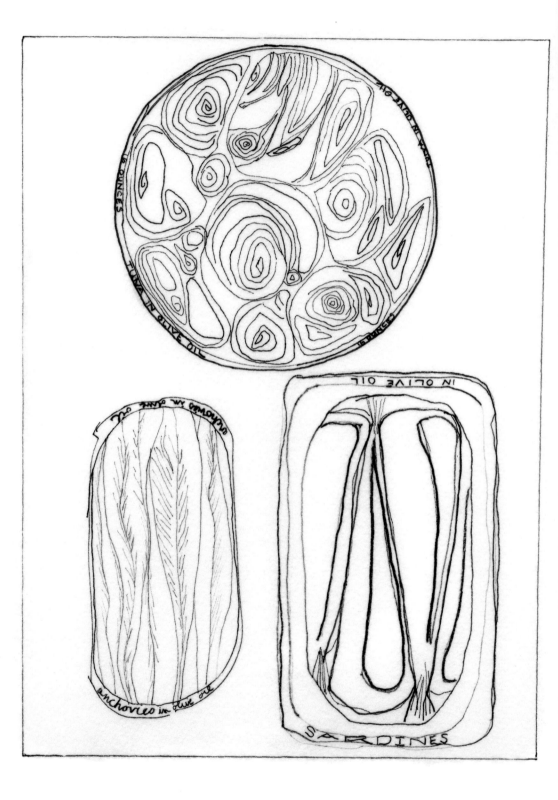

CANNED SARDINES WITH SLICED LEMON

When we were young travelers living on five bucks a day, we always had a couple tins of sardines stashed in our bag for whenever we were really low on funds and got hungry. We still have a taste for them and they come to our rescue when we need a delicious little cracker.

Spread softened salted butter (preferably Irish) on a sturdy cracker (Stoned Wheat Thins, thin Finn Crisps, and original Triscuits are particularly good) and place ½ of a canned sardine packed in olive oil and a paper-thin slice of lemon on top. Add a squeeze of fresh lemon juice and black pepper or red chili flakes. ——*makes 1*

FOR ANCHOVY LOVERS ONLY

We like the simplicity of opening a jar of anchovies packed in oil for these. Though the filets are easier to lift out of a tin, the ones packed in glass tend to have better flavor.

Butter a cracker with softened unsalted butter (preferably Irish). Lay a few (or to your taste) anchovy filets with the oil clinging to them on top. Season with cracked black pepper. A few drops of fresh lemon juice helps cut through the salty richness. Or live it up and add a slice of hard-boiled egg. ——*makes 1*

A CAN OF TUNA & SOME LEMONS

Good canned tuna needs little more than its friend the lemon. We buy the best tuna we can find, always packed in olive oil, usually albacore, *ventresca* (Italian tuna belly), *ventrèche* (the same, but in French), or *bonito* (a dark-fleshed tunalike fish from Spain). We serve it simply: a toothsome hunk of tuna on a cracker or grilled toast with a squeeze of lemon juice. We can't resist big handsome cans (like those 4-pounders) of imported tuna for serving to a crowd. We just pry off the lid, tip out some of the oil, and set it out with lots of crackers or toast and plenty of lemons for everyone to help themselves. Meow! ——*makes 1*

soup's on

❦ A RATIONALE FOR MAKING STOCKS & BROTHS ❦

As convenient as it is to open a can of commercially produced stock, it's never really any good, even those bearing a photograph of a famous chef, in a frozen smile, there on the label. These stocks (chicken is tolerable; beef and vegetable should be avoided at all costs) are imposters, and have little resemblance to a stock you could make yourself. Whether it's a simple quickly made one, using a chicken neck and a handful of chopped vegetables, or a more complicated one, involving an egg-white raft, stocks are the essential building blocks for better soups, stews, braises, sauces, risottos, ragoûts, and so on. We encourage you to make stock and stash in the freezer what you don't use right away. It'll give you a sense of security, all stocked up.

Now let's consider broths. They're like stocks, of course, but richer and more flavorful. They can be eaten (sipped or slurped) alone. As is. Unadorned. When seasoned right, with just enough salt, broth tastes familiar. Like it's part of us. Drinking a bowl (or cup) of warm broth, rich and clear, is a perfect restorative. At Canal House, we often start off meals with a bowl of hot broth, sometimes adding to the pot a big handful of tender spinach leaves, or finely chopped escarole, sliced mushrooms, peas or fresh favas, tiny pastas or fine egg noodles. We like to poach tortellini and ravioli, eggs, tiny meatballs, shrimp, salmon, or cod in broth. So, make broth and drink up—you'll feel glad you did.

❦ There's an old adage, when cooking with wine, to only use what you'd drink. Same thing applies here—a broth will only be as good as its ingredients.

❦ Attending to broth while it simmers on the back burner, skimming off any foam and debris that float to the surface, feels virtuous. But it isn't critical for clarity. The real key is the gentleness of the boil—a few bubbles floating up to the surface every few seconds. A vigorous boil makes a cloudy broth.

❦ We add salt at the very end, after we've strained our broth. Then we can add just as much as we need, depending on how we'll use it.

❦ Fat that accumulates on the broth's surface as it simmers has nice flavor, but sometimes there's too much. Letting the strained broth chill in the refrigerator is the easiest way to get at the fat. As the broth chills, the fat forms a white crust on the surface. Lift off what you don't want. But remember, fat carries lots of flavor, so don't be afraid to leave a little.

BEEF BROTH

This pure, clear blond broth tastes of nothing but beef. We drink it to recuperate. We drink it to maintain a sense of well-being. We use it for soups, braises, stews, and anything calling for meat or beef broth. For this liquid goodness, we have our friend and colleague Julia Lee to thank. It is a staple in her kitchen, an integral component of Korean cuisine.

In the meat department of the grocery store, we often have no choice but to select from what's available. There are times when finding meaty beef bones can be a challenge, so we'll improvise, if necessary, and buy beef marrow bones and a small hunk of chuck. Otherwise, we like to use beef shin and/or neck bones, ultimately looking to use more bone than meat to make this broth.

Put 4–6 pounds meaty beef bones into a large heavy pot. Add enough cold water (about 24 cups) to cover the bones by 2–3 inches. Bring to a rolling boil over high heat, skimming any foam that rises to the surface. Reduce the heat to low and simmer so gently that only a few bubbles gurgle up to the surface every few seconds. Simmer the broth like this, pretty much undisturbed, until it is flavorful, the liquid has reduced by about half, and any meat left on the bones is tender, 5–6 hours. Avoid simmering the broth too actively; it could cloud the otherwise clear liquid.

Strain the broth through a fine sieve into a bowl, discarding the solids. Season with salt. Skim off the top layer of fat if you don't want it. The broth is ready to use, but it can be stored in the refrigerator for a day or two, or frozen for up to 3 months. —— *makes about 12 cups*

TURKEY BROTH
makes about 12 cups

At least once a year we roast a whole turkey, thanks to our beloved Thanksgiving holiday. And when all the feasting is said and done, we throw the carcass, along with any carrot sticks, celery stalks, and the like remaining in the vegetable bin, into a big stock pot and cover it all with water. It simmers away while the dishwasher runs through its last load from the feast.

But the rich flavor of turkey broth is something worth having around at other times of the year. In lieu of roasting a whole bird just to get to the carcass, we buy turkey parts and use those instead—the huge wings are not much money and are just right for the job.

4 whole turkey wings
  (about 7 pounds)
1 tablespoon vegetable oil
1 yellow onion, quartered
1 rib celery, cut in half
1 carrot, peeled and cut in half

½ bunch parsley
2–3 sprigs fresh thyme
1 bay leaf
10 black peppercorns
Salt

Cut the wings into 3 pieces, once at the main joint and again at the tip joint to make them more manageable. Put the oil and wings in a large heavy pot, cover, and cook over medium heat, stirring occasionally to prevent them from browning, until they lose their raw appearance and have released some of their fat and juices, about 20 minutes.

Add the onions, celery, carrots, parsley, thyme, bay leaf, and peppercorns. Add enough cold water (about 24 cups) to cover everything well. Bring to a boil over medium-high heat. Let it boil for about 10 minutes, skimming any foam that floats to the surface. Reduce the heat to medium-low and simmer (gently bubbling) uncovered for about 4 hours. The broth should reduce by about half. Strain the broth through a fine sieve and discard the solids. Season with salt. We like to keep the layer of fat. It adds more flavor to the broth.

CHICKEN BROTH ❧ Follow the directions for making Turkey Broth, substituting 6–8 pounds chicken wings for the turkey wings, and omitting the step of cutting the wings into thirds.

VEGETABLE BROTH
makes about 8 cups

This delicately flavored vegetable broth is given a bit of body by the potato, and its blush from the tomatoes. It is a basic vegetable broth that can be used as you would chicken stock: as a base for soups and risotto, to float little Meatless Meatballs (page 33) or tiny pastas in, or stirring in cooked white beans and a handful of greens. It's fragile, though, and after sitting for a day or so, the broth will separate. Stir it before using and everything will come back together. To add a richer depth of flavor, brown the leeks, celery, carrots, onions, and garlic over higher heat without covering the pot.

2 tablespoons olive or vegetable oil
3 leeks, trimmed, washed, and
 coarsely chopped
3 ribs celery, coarsely chopped
3 carrots, peeled and coarsely chopped
1 yellow onion, coarsely chopped
4–6 cloves garlic, peeled
One 28-ounce can whole peeled
 plum tomatoes

1 medium all-purpose white
 potato, peeled and quartered
1 bunch parsley
2–3 sprigs fresh thyme
2 bay leaves
10 black peppercorns
Salt

Heat the oil in a large heavy pot over medium heat. Add the leeks, celery, carrots, onions, and garlic. Cover the pot and cook the vegetables, stirring occasionally to prevent them from browning, until softened, about 20 minutes.

Add the tomatoes and their juices, potatoes, parsley, thyme, bay leaves, peppercorns, and 16 cups cold water to the pot. Bring to a boil over medium-high heat. Reduce the heat to medium and simmer uncovered for 30–40 minutes. Strain the broth through a fine sieve and discard the solids.

Return the broth to the pot. Season it with salt—it will likely need a good bit of it. Simmer over medium heat, uncovered, until reduced by half, about 1 hour. The broth will keep in a sealed container or plastic bag for up to 2 days in the refrigerator or up to 6 months in the freezer.

MEATLESS MEATBALLS IN BROTH

This simple soup, which relies on using a richly flavored broth—beef, poultry, or vegetable (see pages 29–31)—is loosely based on the components of the classic soup from Emilia-Romagna, passatelli. It is one of our favorites.

Mix 1 cup freshly grated parmigiano-reggiano, 3–4 tablespoons fine dry plain bread crumbs, finely grated zest of 1 lemon, 1 tablespoon chopped fresh parsley, and 1 egg in a small mixing bowl into a soft dough. Bring 6 cups flavorful broth to a simmer over medium heat. Roll pea-size pieces of the dough into balls. Add the little balls to the simmering broth and cook until slightly swollen and cooked through, about 3 minutes. —— *serves 4*

SWISS CHARD & LEMON SOUP
serves 4–6

Use any of the sturdy greens, like collards or kale, to make this soup. Dark leafy greens are loaded with potassium and vitamins A and C, and we all need as much of those as we can get. We throw in a handful of raisins to add a touch of sweetness and preserved lemon rind for a little tartness.

3 tablespoons extra-virgin olive oil
1 large yellow onion, chopped
1 clove garlic, minced
2 bunches young Swiss chard, stems and leaves chopped separately
⅓ cup raisins

Rind of ½ preserved lemon, minced
Salt and pepper
5 cups turkey or chicken broth (page 30)
1 cup cooked ditalini
Really good extra-virgin olive oil

Heat the oil in a large pot over medium heat. Add the onions and garlic and cook, stirring occasionally, until just tender, about 10 minutes. Add the chard stems, raisins, and preserved lemon, cover, and continue cooking for about 10 minutes.

Add the Swiss chard leaves, season with salt and pepper, cover, and continue cooking until the leaves have wilted, about 10 minutes. Add the broth, cover, and cook for 15 minutes. Add the ditalini and serve with a drizzle of really good extra-virgin olive oil.

Left: Swiss Chard & Lemon Soup

BROTHY BEEF SHORT RIBS
serves 4

There are a few cuts of beef that are particularly well suited for boiling, beef short ribs is one of them. It takes a while for the meat to become tender, but while it simmers, it releases its rich beefy flavor without drying out like some pieces of beef can. The meat is as enjoyable to eat, sprinkled with salt, as it is to drink its flavorful ginger-infused broth, which may just be an aphrodisiac.

3–4 pounds beef short ribs
1 hand-size piece fresh ginger, unpeeled, halved crosswise
2–3 cloves garlic, optional

Salt
1 bunch fresh cilantro, chopped
2–3 scallions, chopped

Put the short ribs, ginger, and garlic, if using, into a large heavy pot and add enough cold water (about 16 cups) to cover the meat by 2–3 inches. Bring to a boil over medium-high heat, skimming any foam that rises to the surface. Reduce the heat to low and simmer very gently until the meat is tender, about 5 hours.

Remove and discard the ginger and garlic and any loose bones. Season the broth with salt. Trim any fat and gristle from the meat. Serve the meat and broth in deep soup bowls, garnished with lots of cilantro and scallions. Pass salt around the table for seasoning the beef.

BROTHY BEEF SHORT RIBS & ROOT VEGETABLES ❦ Follow the directions above for boiled beef short ribs, omitting the ginger in the first step. One hour before the meat is finished cooking, add 2 each quartered and peeled carrots, parsnips, and turnips to the simmering broth. Substitute a half bunch fresh parsley leaves, chopped, for the cilantro and scallions at the end.

SMOKED FISH STEW

We'd spent a week on the road eating our way through Ireland and got back to Dublin in time for one last meal before flying out the next morning. We landed a table for two at The Winding Stair restaurant above the venerable bookshop of the same name after begging them to squeeze us in anywhere. The place was packed when we arrived. Taking us at our word, they seated us in a tight corner at a coffee table with our backs to the room and a bookshelf before us. But after the first spoonfuls of a seafood stew of Nicholson's hand-smoked haddock, poached in milk with onions and white Cheddar mash, we felt we had the best seats in the house. Inspired, now we make our own version of the stew.

Melt 4 tablespoons butter in a large heavy pot over medium heat. Add 3 thickly sliced washed, trimmed leeks. Cook until softened but not browned, 10–15 minutes. Add 3 thickly sliced peeled russet potatoes and 6 cups whole milk. Gently simmer until potatoes are tender, about 30 minutes. Meanwhile, carefully remove the skin and bones from 1 pound smoked whitefish without breaking up the pieces of fish too much. Place fish in a medium pot, add 2 cups whole milk, and heat over medium-low heat until warm. Fry 6 ounces diced salt pork in a skillet over medium heat until crisp, 5–10 minutes. Drain on paper towels. Carefully add fish and milk to the pot with the potatoes. Serve stew garnished with lots of chopped scallions and the salt pork. ——*serves 6*

CLAM CHOWDER
serves 4

We always keep everything on hand to make this simple chowder.

3 tablespoons butter
2 ribs celery, diced small
1 small yellow onion, chopped
1 clove garlic, minced
2 tablespoons flour
2 cups whole milk
One 8-ounce bottle clam juice

One 10-ounce can whole baby clams
2 small all-purpose white potatoes, peeled and cut into small cubes
1 bay leaf
Leaves from 1 sprig fresh thyme
Salt and pepper

Melt the butter in a medium pot over medium-low heat. Add the celery, onions, and garlic and cook, stirring occasionally, until soft, 15–20 minutes. Add the flour, stirring constantly to prevent it from browning, and cook for 1–2 minutes. Gradually whisk in the milk and clam juice.

Add the clams and their juice, potatoes, bay leaf, and thyme. Season to taste with salt and pepper. Simmer over medium to medium-low heat, stirring often, until potatoes are tender and the soup has thickened, about 30 minutes.

QUICK CIOPPINO
serves 4–6

This San Francisco seafood masterpiece was made by Genoese immigrant fisherman who fished the rich waters of the bay. Usually made with Dungeness crab, often right on the fishing boat, the soup varied with each day's catch. Our quick version defies locale and season and relies instead on the freezer section—and it's delicious.

¼ cup extra-virgin olive oil
1 small yellow onion, finely chopped
1 rib celery, finely chopped
½ bulb fennel, finely chopped
2 cloves garlic, minced
1 large pinch peperoncini
1 cup white or red wine
3½ cups tomato juice

One 10-ounce can whole baby clams
2 bay leaves
1 teaspoon chopped fresh thyme
12 ounces frozen mixed seafood, such as bay scallops, peeled shrimp, and calamari rings, thawed
8 ounces cod filet
2 tablespoons chopped parsley
Really good extra-virgin olive oil

Heat the oil in a medium pot over medium-high heat. Add the onions, celery, fennel, garlic, and peperoncini and cook until vegetables just begin to brown, 5–7 minutes. Add the wine and cook until reduced by half. Add the tomato juice, clams plus their juice, bay leaves, and thyme and bring to a boil. Reduce the heat to medium and simmer, stirring occasionally, until soup has reduced by about a quarter, 10–15 minutes. Add the seafood and fish, and simmer until just cooked through, 6–8 minutes. Remove and discard the bay leaves. Stir in the parsley and serve with a good drizzle of really good extra-virgin olive oil.

eat your vegetables

ASPARAGUS & COMPANY

When local asparagus arrive here in the Northeast, it's a spring sensation, and we feast on the fat gnarly spears until they dwindle out, sometime toward the beginning of July. We can afford to be choosy when they're in season, so we buy only spears with tightly closed tips and moist ends.

Soak 1 pound fat asparagus in a few changes of cold water to help rid them of any sandy grit. Lay the spears flat on a cutting board to keep them from snapping, and peel off their skins up to the tips, using a sharp swivel-blade vegetable peeler. Trim off the woody ends with a sharp knife. Bring a pot of water to a boil over medium-high heat and generously season with salt. Cook the asparagus in the boiling water until tender, 4–5 minutes. Lift the asparagus out of the water with a slotted spatula and drain on a clean dish cloth. Serve the asparagus hot with either of the delicious butters below. —— *serves 2–4*

BLENDER LEMON-BUTTER SAUCE

Put 4 large egg yolks, ¼ cup fresh lemon juice, a big pinch of salt, and pepper to taste into the jar of an electric blender. Cover and blend for 1 minute. With the motor still running, gradually add 8 tablespoons warm melted butter in a slow steady stream through the hole in the blender lid, leaving any milky solids behind. Adjust seasonings. Serve with asparagus. —— *makes 1 cup*

FAVORITE ASPARAGUS BUTTER

Put a generous spoonful of softened Anchovy & Lemon Butter (page 18) on each of 2–4 plates and put the hot asparagus spears on top. Garnish each plate with a big wedge of lemon. —— *serves 2–4*

ASPARAGUS FRITTATA

Often simple is sublime. Trim and peel 1 pound asparagus (see above). Blanch the asparagus in a pot of salted boiling water over high heat for 2 minutes. Drain and set aside on paper towels. Beat together 6 eggs,

¼ cup grated parmigiano-reggiano, and a big pinch of salt and black pepper. Drizzle a few tablespoons of good olive oil into a large ovenproof nonstick skillet over medium heat. Add 2 thinly sliced garlic cloves and the asparagus, and cook for about 3 minutes. Pour the eggs into the skillet and cook, lifting the edges to allow any uncooked egg to flow underneath the cooked, until the frittata is almost set. Add a sprinkling of parmigiano-reggiano and put the skillet under a preheated broiler until the frittata is lightly browned, 1–2 minutes. Serve with lemon wedges. ——*serves 4*

ASPARAGUS RISOTTO
serves 4

By adding the asparagus tips at the very end, they will keep their pretty shape and their bright green flavor.

6 tablespoons butter
1 onion, finely chopped
1 clove garlic, minced
Salt and pepper
1 cup carnaroli, vialone nano,
   or arborio rice
¼ cup white wine

6 cups hot chicken broth (page 30)
12 spears asparagus, peeled,
   tips reserved, spears chopped
Grated zest of ½ lemon
Juice of 1 lemon
½ cup grated parmigiano-reggiano

Melt the butter in a large heavy pan over medium heat. Add the onions and garlic and season with salt and pepper. Cook, stirring with a wooden spoon, until the onions and garlic are soft but not browned, about 5 minutes.

Add the rice to the pan and stir until it is coated with the butter and onions. Pour in the wine and stir until the rice has absorbed it, about 5 minutes.

Add the chicken broth 1 cup at a time, stirring often and only adding more when the rice has absorbed the broth. After you add the fourth cup of broth, add the chopped asparagus spears, lemon zest, and lemon juice. Continue cooking and adding broth until the rice is just tender and still a little soupy. Remove from heat, add the asparagus tips, cover, and allow to rest for about 5 minutes. Stir in the cheese and more butter, if you like.

Overleaf: left, thin and fat asparagus; right, asparagus with Blender Lemon-Butter Sauce

BROCCOLI RABE & CHORIZO
serves 4

Many recipes suggest blanching broccoli rabe (also known as rapini) in boiling water before sautéing or stewing in order to tame the taste. But we like its slightly bitter, pungent, green flavor. So we just chop and go! Serve this as a vegetable, or chop the broccoli rabe a little finer and toss it in long strands of cooked pasta. D'Artagnan, a gourmet food purveyor, sells fresh Spanish chorizo (6 to the pound) in many grocery stores.

2 fresh chorizo sausages,
   about 6 ounces
¼ cup good extra-virgin olive oil
1 clove garlic, sliced

1 big pinch peperoncini
1 pound broccoli rabe
Salt and pepper

Remove the casing from the sausages and discard. Finely chop the sausages. Heat the oil in a large skillet over medium-high heat. Add the garlic, peperoncini, and chorizo, and cook, stirring with a wooden spoon, for about 2 minutes.

Trim and discard the ends from the broccoli rabe, then rinse in cold water. Chop the broccoli rabe and add to the skillet with water still clinging to its leaves. Stir to mix eveything together, and cook until the broccoli rabe is tender, about 5 minutes. Season with salt and pepper, and a nice drizzle of really good extra-virgin olive oil, if you like.

JANSSON'S TEMPTATION
serves 4

This Scandinavian classic combines anchovies and potatoes and is one of our favorite recipes. We use Consorcio Anchovy Filets from Corti Brothers (page 7) or instead, use the highest quality oil-packed anchovies that you can find.

6 tablespoons butter
1 cup fresh bread crumbs
One 2-ounce tin anchovies in oil
1 large yellow onion, thinly sliced

1 pound russet potatoes, peeled
Salt
4 tablespoons heavy cream
Pepper

Preheat oven to 375°. Melt 4 tablespoons of the butter in a medium pan over medium-high heat. Add bread crumbs and mix until well coated. Transfer to a bowl. In the same pan, add 2 more tablespoons of the butter and the anchovies and their oil and cook, stirring with a wooden spoon, until the anchovies have melted. Add onions and cook until soft and lightly golden, about 15 minutes.

While the onions cook, thinly slice the potatoes, then parboil in a pot of boiling salted water over high heat, for 5 minutes. Drain. Arrange a layer of potatoes in the bottom of a buttered baking dish. Spoon 2 tablespoons of the cream over the potatoes and season with pepper. Spread onions over the potatoes. Layer remaining potatoes. Spoon remaining 2 tablespoons of cream over the potatoes and season with salt and pepper. Sprinkle the reserved bread crumbs on top. Bake until the potatoes are tender, 20–25 minutes.

CAULIFLOWER WITH TOASTED SPICED BREAD CRUMBS
serves 6

Make extra of the delicious, warm-flavored fennel spice mix. It's good to have on hand to sprinkle on chicken or fish before roasting.

For FENNEL SPICE MIX
2 tablespoons fennel seeds
6 black peppercorns
2 pinches red pepper flakes

¾ cup extra-virgin olive oil
2 cups fresh plain bread crumbs
Salt
1 head cauliflower, deeply cored keeping the head intact

For the Fennel Spice Mix, toast fennel seeds and peppercorns in a dry skillet over medium heat until fragrant, 3–4 minutes. Finely crush them with the red pepper flakes in a mortar and pestle.

Heat ½ cup of the oil in a large skillet over medium heat until warm. Add bread crumbs and half the Fennel Spice Mix. Toast the bread crumbs, stirring frequently, until deep golden brown and crunchy, 4–5 minutes. Remove from heat. Season with salt and more spices to taste. Cook the cauliflower in a large pot of salted boiling water over medium heat until tender, about 10 minutes. Drain in a colander, then place on a platter flower side up. Spoon bread crumbs over and around the cauliflower. Drizzle with remaining ¼ cup oil.

Overleaf: left, broccoli rabe (rapini); right, Broccoli Rabe & Chorizo

❦ IN PRAISE OF ESCAROLE ❦
(the cooked & the raw)

By now you probably know that we sometimes get on a jag about an ingredient, cooking and eating it and nothing else. In the past couple of years, we've been smitten with anchovies and bread crumbs, intoxicated by preserved lemons and marmalades, and just plain crazy for chives and scallions. Whether it's a flavor or a way of preparing food, it eventually gives way to the new next thing, but it's never lost or forgotten. It simply becomes part of our repertoire.

Well, we've been on an escarole jag that just won't quit. As far as chicories and endives go, escarole isn't the prettiest member of the family. Its outer green leaves are ragged and coarse. And it has a bit of a bitter reputation. But we just remove all those dark green leaves, cut off the darkest green tips, and use only the delicately toothsome, mildly bitter, pretty, pale green-tinged inner yellow leaves.

The beauty of escarole is that it is equally good eaten cooked or raw. We sauté wet leaves in olive oil with garlic until the escarole is just supple. Then we pile it onto pieces of crusty toast; stir it into long strands of cooked spaghetti or orecchiette; top it with a big spoonful of fresh ricotta, lots of good extra-virgin olive oil, and cracked black pepper; crush some canned plum tomatoes into the skillet and stew them together briefly; eat it alongside pan-fried or grilled sausages, loin lamb chops, or a fat steak; add handfuls of cooked peas and serve it with fish or chicken; or add some heavy cream, grate Asiago cheese over it, and brown it under the broiler for a quick gratin. We braise escarole with chicken, fish, or cooked dried white beans. We make classic Italian soups with it. And we add it, coarsely chopped, to a simmering rich broth and eat it just like that.

Raw, it has replaced Bibb lettuce as our everyday leafy green for salads, tossed with a lemony vinaigrette. It has just the right crunch. It's delicious with canned tuna, pieces of cold leftover chicken, and piled on top of a pan-fried cutlet—veal, chicken, or pork. And, no kidding, it's really good with anchovies, toasted buttery bread crumbs, even a little chopped preserved lemon. With escarole, you could say we're going steady.

BRAISED ESCAROLE WITH WHITE BEANS
serves 2

Escarole always needs a good soak in cold water to rid it of the dirt trapped between its leaves. We wash it just before preparing this classic Italian dish so that the leaves still have water clinging to them when they are added to the skillet. This way, when they meet the warm oil they wilt gently instead of frying. Either of the smaller variety of dried white beans—navy or great Northern—work just as well as the more traditional cannellini here.

1 head escarole, dark green outer leaves discarded, inner leaves separated and trimmed of dark green tops

¼ cup good extra-virgin olive oil

1–2 cloves garlic, thinly sliced

1–2 cups cooked white beans with some of their cooking liquid or a small ladleful of water (page 67)

Salt and pepper

Wash the escarole leaves well and shake off some of the water. Put the olive oil and garlic into a large nonreactive skillet and warm over medium heat until fragrant, about 1 minute. Add the escarole and cook briefly, turning the leaves as they begin to wilt. Add the beans and their cooking liquid or water, season with salt and pepper, and braise just until the beans are warmed through and the escarole is still bright and colorful, 3–5 minutes.

ESCAROLE SALAD WITH LEMON & PARMESAN

Use the best olive oil you can find to make this salad. You can make nice thin shavings of cheese using a swivel-blade vegetable peeler. Mash together ½ clove garlic and a pinch of salt with the back of a wooden spoon in a salad bowl. Stir in the diced rind of ¼ preserved lemon and the juice of ½ lemon. Whisk in ¼ cup really good extra-virgin olive oil, adding more to suit yourself. Toss 4–6 cups dry, trimmed, washed, tender escarole leaves with the vinaigrette. Serve the salad garnished with plenty of thin shavings of parmigiano-reggiano and some cracked black pepper. —— *serves 2–4*

Overleaf: left, Braised Escarole with White Beans; right, Escarole Salad with Lemon & Parmesan

CREAMED SPINACH
serves 2–4

Potatoes thicken this creamy spinach, and ginger brightens its green flavor.

FOR THE GINGER-GARLIC PASTE
One 5-inch finger fresh ginger,
 peeled and chopped
6 cloves garlic
Salt
Really good extra-virgin olive oil

FOR THE SPINACH
3 tablespoons butter
1 potato, peeled and diced
Salt and pepper
¼ cup heavy cream
1 pound washed young spinach

For the Ginger-Garlic Paste, pulse the ginger, garlic, and a pinch of salt in a food processor or blender until smooth. Add a little water to thin the paste. Store in a covered container with a little olive oil on the surface. Keeps for about a week.

For the spinach, melt the butter in a large pot over medium heat. Add 1 big tablespoon Ginger-Garlic Paste and cook for a minute, swirling it in the butter. Add the potatoes and stir until well coated. Season with salt and pepper. Reduce heat to medium-low, cover, and cook until tender but not browned, about 10 minutes.

Add the cream and pile the spinach into the pot, pressing it down so that you can fit it all in. Cover and cook until the spinach wilts, about 10 minutes. Fold the spinach into the potatoes and cream, and serve.

SPINACH FLAN
serves 4

Perfect for a savory breakfast, or for lunch with a glass of Petite Arvine, that lovely Italian white, or as supper when you've forgotten to defrost the lamb chops.

3 tablespoons butter
4 ounces shallots (about 6), peeled
 and halved lengthwise
Salt and pepper
Freshly grated nutmeg

1 pound washed young spinach
1½ cups half-and-half
3 eggs
4 ounces Gruyère, grated

Preheat the oven to 325°. Melt the butter in an ovenproof pan over medium heat. Add the shallots and keeping the halves intact, cook until soft, about 15 minutes. Season with salt and pepper and nutmeg.

Put the spinach in a colander fitted over a pot of boiling water, cover, and steam until the spinach has wilted, 5–10 minutes.

Beat the half-and-half and eggs together in a small bowl. Transfer spinach to the pan with the shallots. Pour the eggs over and around the spinach. Scatter the cheese evenly on top. Bake for 20 minutes, then slide under the broiler until golden, about 1 minute.

STEAMED SPINACH

We are fiends for cooked spinach bathed in butter. Who knows, maybe we're iron-deficient—we're not! We just can't get enough of it. We cook the leaves by steaming them until they wilt and collapse into suppleness. Because we're not boiling them, we eliminate the problem of waterlogged leaves, and there's no need to squeeze out the liquid—which delicate young spinach can't handle.

Put 10–12 ounces tender young washed spinach leaves in a colander or steamer basket and set it over a pot of gently boiling water (don't let the bottom of the colander or steamer basket touch the water). Cover and steam, turning the leaves a few times as they wilt, until tender, about 5 minutes. Serve spinach while still hot, adding 2–4 tablespoons softened butter and salt and pepper to taste. — *serves 2*

POACHED EGGS

We serve these eggs right on top of our steamed spinach and with our cooked asparagus (page 40). They're also good slipped into a bowl of hot broth (page 30) and added to a dish of warm cooked dried beans (page 67). Fill a medium pan with water and bring it to a simmer. Crack 2 eggs into 2 small cups. Stir the water well, then tip 1 egg at a time into the center of the swirling water. Simmer the eggs over medium-low heat until the whites are white and the yolks remain soft, about 3 minutes. Lift the eggs from the water with a slotted spoon and drain on a clean dish cloth. Serve with a big knob of butter and salt and pepper on top, if you like. — *makes 2*

Overleaf: left, Creamed Spinach; right, young spinach

PEAS & POTATOES

Peas go great with just about everything. Quality frozen organic peas are pretty darn good. Of course, when fresh peas arrive in the market, we are happy to sit and shuck away, but before they show up and after they make their brief appearance, we do rely on the freezer to help us get our daily requirement.

A 10-ounce bag of frozen peas feeds two hungry people very nicely. We put them in a pot with a couple of tablespoons of water and a big or little knob of butter, depending on how virtuous we are feeling, cover the pot, and simmer over medium heat for about 3 minutes, just until they're done. Then we add boiled potatoes, crumbled cooked bacon, and always lots of chopped chives or mint or both. ——*serves 2*

LILLIE'S PASTA WITH PEAS & HAM

Sometimes we are lucky enough to have children come to hang out with us at Canal House. On one such occasion, Lillie Anderson—who in past visits acted as a self-appointed tea-girl, serving us cups of sweet, milky tea and cold dill pickles—expanded her repertoire and whipped up this lovely little lunch for us. So simple even a child can make it!

Cook 1 pound rigatoni in a large pot of salted boiling water over high heat until just tender, 12–14 minutes. While the pasta cooks, finely chop ¼–½ pound boiled ham. Drain the cooked pasta, then return it to the pot, add 1 cup half-and-half, ¼ cup grated parmigiano–reggiano, and a 10-ounce package frozen sweet peas. Cook over medium heat, stirring occasionally to keep the pasta from sticking to the bottom of the pot, until the peas are cooked, about 3 minutes. Season with salt and pepper to taste. Divide the pasta between 4–6 plates and garnish with the chopped ham and lots of finely chopped chives. ——*serves 4–6*

CUTLETS SMOTHERED IN PEAS

Everyone relies on cutlets—boneless, skinless chicken breasts or those little pork tenderloins that you slice—when they need to get dinner on the table quickly, which is more often than not. We certainly do. Sometimes we season cutlets with salt and pepper, then sear them in a little olive oil; other times we dip them in beaten egg, then in panko, and quickly fry them. Either way, we love to smother them with peas.

Melt 4 tablespoons butter in a medium pot. Add a 16-ounce bag frozen peas and 1 bunch trimmed chopped scallions, cover, and cook until peas are tender. Season well with salt and pepper and add more butter, if you like. Put the seared or fried cutlets on plates, then spoon the peas on top. —— *serves 4*

MEZZI RIGATONI WITH PEAS & RICOTTA

The cute fat mezzi rigatoni provide the perfect hiding places for sweet baby peas and scallions. Italian grocery stores sell good-quality fresh ricotta.

Cook 1 pound mezzi rigatoni in a large pot of boiling salted water until just tender, 12–14 minutes. Drain the pasta in a colander, leaving about ¼ cup of the pasta water in the pot. Return the pot to the stove. Add ¼ cup really good extra-virgin olive oil, 1 pound frozen baby peas, and 6 thinly sliced scallions and cook over medium heat for about 1 minute. Season to taste with salt and pepper. Remove about 1 cup of the peas and scallions and set aside. Add the pasta back to the pot and toss everything together. Taste and adjust the seasonings. Transfer the pasta to a platter and spoon 2 cups ricotta over the pasta. Spoon the reserved peas and scallions on top of the ricotta. Drizzle with more really good extra-virgin olive oil and season with salt and pepper. —— *serves 4–8*

I eat my peas with honey; I've done it all my life. It makes the peas taste funny, but it keeps them on the knife. —— Anonymous

"FRESH" PEA SOUP
makes 6 cups

We use organic frozen sweet peas to make this beautiful bright-green soup. Adding them to the pot at the tail end of the cooking time preserves their sweet flavor and vivid green color. It's lovely garnished with lots of snipped fresh chives, dill, or chervil. Adding a small dollop of crème fraîche, sour cream, or whipped cream to each serving is pretty delicious, too.

2 tablespoons butter

1 leek, trimmed, washed, and sliced

1 russet potato, peeled and cut into small pieces

4 cups chicken broth (page 30)

2 pounds (6 cups) frozen peas

Salt and pepper

Melt the butter in a medium pot over medium heat. Add the leeks and cook, stirring often, until soft but not colored, about 10 minutes.

Add the potatoes and chicken broth to the pot and cook until the potatoes are tender, about 20 minutes. Add the peas and season with some salt and pepper. When the peas are heated through, about 1 minute, remove the pot from the heat.

Working in batches, purée the soup in a blender. For a smoother texture, pass it through a strainer into a bowl, discarding the solids. Taste the soup and season it with more salt, if you like, as it will probably need it.

Return the soup to the pot and warm it over low heat. Or, cover and refrigerate it until cold. Serve the soup hot or cold.

SUCCOTASH

The rather plain combination of starchy limas and corn is one of those old-fashioned flavors we're so fond of. We make it with frozen vegetables when fresh summer ones aren't available. We toss in some bright green peas (yes, the frozen kind) to add color and a little *variety*.

Bring a pot of salted water to a boil over medium-high heat. Add 1 cup frozen baby lima beans and 1 cup frozen tender white sweet corn kernels and cook for 3–4 minutes. Add ½ cup frozen baby sweet peas and cook for 1–2 minutes. Drain all but just a bit of the cooking water. Return the succotash to the pot and add 4 tablespoons salted butter (preferably Irish) and season with salt and cracked black pepper. —— *serves 2–4*

BABY LIMAS WITH FETA

The pleasantly dull (and we mean this in the nicest way) flavor of lima beans is a good foil for the tangy saltiness of feta. There are so many varieties of feta to choose from at the grocery store. We like the creamy mildness of French feta, but use what you like.

Bring a pot of salted water to a boil over medium-high heat. Add 2 cups frozen baby lima beans and cook for 4–5 minutes. Drain. Put the warm limas in a serving dish, lay a thin slice of feta on top, and drizzle with ¼ cup or more really good extra-virgin olive oil. Season with cracked black pepper. Sometimes we add thin slices of red onion. —— *serves 4*

FAVAS & PEAS SALAD
serves 6–8

We cheat and get a little jump on spring when using frozen favas and peas for this salad.

Salt

1 pound frozen peas

One 28-ounce bag frozen fava beans

½ cup extra-virgin olive oil

2–3 cloves garlic, thinly sliced

4 ounces prosciutto, finely diced

4 scallions, chopped

Juice of 1 lemon

½ bunch mint, leaves thinly sliced

Pepper

Bring a medium pot of salted water to a boil over high heat. Put the peas in a large sieve, submerge it in the boiling water, and blanch the peas for 15–30 seconds. Rinse them under cold water; set aside. Blanch the favas for 1 minute. Drain and plunge them into a bowl of cold water. Drain again and peel off and discard the tough outer skins. Put the tender bright green favas into a bowl.

Warm the oil and garlic in a small pan over medium-low heat until the garlic is soft, about 5 minutes. Put the peas, favas, and prosciutto on a serving platter. Pour the warm garlic oil over the favas and peas. Add the scallions, lemon juice, and mint. Season with salt and pepper. Garnish with lemon, if you like.

FAVA MASH

We just can't say enough about favas. We know they can be a royal pain to peel, but peel them you must, as the skins are tough and unpleasant. There is nothing quite like those sweet little beans with their rich flavor and dense starchy texture. We serve this mash on little toasts with olive oil and salt. Or, we use it as a thin bed for grilled chicken or spread on top of poached fish. You get the idea—basically it's good on or under just about anything.

Use a fork to mash together cooked peeled favas, minced garlic, really good extra-virgin olive oil, and salt and pepper. For a smoother texture purée it in a food processor instead. Add a squeeze of fresh lemon juice, if you like. —— *make as much as you like*

Left: Favas & Peas Salad

STEAMED RICE
makes 3 cups

This recipe can easily be doubled—that way you'll have enough for one meal, and enough leftover to make Fried Rice (page 63) another day.

1 cup long-grain rice
½ teaspoon salt

Put the rice into a bowl, cover it with cold water, and swish it around with your hand. The water will turn cloudy. Drain the rice in a sieve, return it to the bowl, and repeat the rinsing process until the water remains clear, 3–4 more times. Drain the rice and transfer it to a heavy medium pot with a tight-fitting lid.

Add 1½ cups cold water and the salt to the pot. Bring to a boil over medium-high heat and cook, uncovered and undisturbed, until the water has evaporated just to the surface of the rice, about 2½ minutes. Reduce the heat slightly if the bubbling water prevents you from seeing the water level. Reduce the heat to low, cover the pot, and cook until the water is completely absorbed and the rice is tender and dry, 10–15 minutes. Let rice rest for 5–10 minutes, covered, then fluff it with a fork.

FRIED RICE
makes 4 cups

When we order in Chinese food (or is that called "take out"?), there's inevitably a container of leftover rice. We refrigerate it and use the cold grains to make our own fried rice. But it is much better when we use our own rice. Sometimes we make it just to have it left over. This recipe isn't as loaded up as some versions we get from our local Chinese restaurant—ours just has ham, peas and egg—but we like it like that.

2 tablespoons vegetable oil
1 clove garlic, minced
3 cups cold cooked long-grain rice (page 62)
½ cup diced ham
½ cup frozen peas, thawed

2 teaspoons Asian sesame oil
1 egg, beaten
1 tablespoon oyster sauce
2 teaspoons soy sauce
2 teaspoons chili garlic sauce, optional

Heat the oil in a wok or large nonstick skillet over medium heat. Add the garlic and cook until fragrant, about 10 seconds. Add the rice and cook, breaking up any clumps with the back of a wooden spoon and stirring the grains to separate them, for 2–3 minutes. Add the ham and peas and continue to cook, stirring frequently, until they are heated through, about 1 minute.

Push the rice out to the sides of the wok. Add the sesame oil to the center, then add the egg and scramble it as it cooks until just set, 30–45 seconds. Add the oyster sauce, soy sauce, and chili garlic sauce, if using, and stir-fry until well combined, about 1 minute.

❧ NOTES ON DRIED BEANS ❧

We cook beans all the time, but we do it instinctively. To verify that our methods are up to scratch, we asked our colleague Julia Lee to dive in and do a little bean research. Turns out our instincts were right. Here's what she found out.

BUYING ❧ Choose beans that have been recently harvested and dried; this may be the most important factor in cooking a good pot of dried beans. As beans age, their outer shell becomes tough and impermeable. Sometimes really old beans will never get tender, even after hours and hours of cooking. Shop at a store that moves a lot of beans off their shelves, ensuring that you're buying from a current crop. Though it may be hard to spot, look for an expiration date on the package.

SOAKING ❧ To soak or not to soak, that is the question. Soaking hydrates and softens the dried beans, giving them a jump start. But you have to think ahead and remember to soak them in the first place. If you choose to soak your beans, they only need about 4 hours (the oft-used phrase "soak the beans overnight" is more about convenience). Or you can use the "quick" soak method: put the beans in a pot, cover them with cold water, bring the water to a boil, and remove the pot from heat. Cover the pot and let the beans soak for 1 hour. Drain, then cover the beans with fresh cold water and gently simmer them until tender. This method will shorten the cooking time a bit and leach out some of the indigestible carbohydrates that cause flatulence (unfortunately, some of the beneficial vitamins and minerals will also get poured down the drain). If you forgo soaking, just put the unsoaked beans right in a pot, cover with cold water, and onto the stove they go. But be sure that you cook them at the gentlest simmer so their skins don't break.

SALTING ❧ Kitchen lore has it that adding salt to beans while they cook will inhibit them from ever becoming tender, but it's just not true. In fact, salt accelerates the cooking time by tenderizing the bean skins.

COOKING ❧ For plump, creamy beans that hold their shape, cook them slowly over low heat in plenty of water. See our recipe for cooked beans on the next page.

Overleaf: left, pots of beans; right, Lentils with Roasted Beets

66

BASIC COOKED DRIED BEANS
makes 6 cups

It is your preference whether to soak or not to soak. MH likes to hydrate the beans before cooking; CH believes that with the gentlest cooking you can jump right in without a soak.

2 cups dried beans, unsoaked or soaked for 4 hours or overnight

1–2 cloves garlic

1 branch fresh thyme, optional

2 bay leaves

Salt

Drain the beans and put them into a medium, heavy-bottomed pot. Cover them with cold water by 2 inches or so. Add the garlic, thyme, if using, and bay leaves. Bring the beans just to a simmer over medium heat, stirring occasionally. Reduce the heat to low and very gently simmer them until they are swollen and tender, 30–90 minutes (or more), depending on the freshness of the dried beans. Remove the pot from the heat. Stir in a generous pinch of salt. Let the beans cool to just warm or to room temperature in the cooking liquid. (The beans will keep in the refrigerator for up to 4 days.)

LENTILS WITH ROASTED BEETS

Earthy beets and lentils were made for each other—dirt on dirt in the very best sort of way.

Preheat the oven to 375°. Wrap 4 small beets individually in aluminum foil and put them in a baking pan. Roast the beets until tender, about 1 hour. While the beets roast, rinse 1½ cups lentils in cold water. Put the lentils in a medium pot with 3 cups water, 1 small peeled onion, 2 garlic cloves, and 1 bay leaf. Bring to a boil over medium heat, reduce heat to low, and gently simmer until all the water has been absorbed and the lentils are tender, about 1 hour. Add more water if you need to. Use a slotted spoon to fish out the onion, garlic, and bay leaf. Remove the beets from the oven, unwrap, and when cool enough to handle, slip off the skins. Dice the beets, then add them to the lentils. Season to taste with salt and pepper. Transfer to a serving dish and drizzle generously with a really good extra-virgin olive oil, and garnish with lots of chopped parsley and scallions. —*serves 6*

BLACK BEAN SOUP
serves 6

Every day in Havana, pots of black beans simmer gently on back burners of old stoves. We visited there some years ago and we never forgot the black bean soup our hostesses, Mariana and Magdelena, served for lunch—long-simmered, silky black beans with pieces of spicy chorizo and a golden sofrito of onions and garlic swirled in near the end of cooking. We like to serve it with a scoop of fragrant white rice.

1 pound dried black beans

One large sprig fresh oregano, or 1 teaspoon dried oregano

1 large bay leaf

Extra-virgin olive oil

1 tablespoon ground cumin

1 white onion, finely chopped

2 cloves garlic, sliced

12 scallions, finely chopped, plus more for garnish

Salt and pepper

2 Spanish-style chorizo sausages, coarsely chopped

Fresh cilantro leaves

Lime wedges

Rinse the beans under cold running water. Put the beans, oregano, bay leaf, and about 1 tablespoon olive oil into a large heavy pot, then cover with cold water by 3 inches. Bring to a boil over medium heat, then reduce heat to low, and simmer, adding more water as needed to keep beans covered, until beans are tender, about 2 hours.

Heat about 3 tablespoons oil in a medium skillet over medium heat. Add the cumin, onions, garlic, and scallions, and sauté, stirring often, until onions are soft and golden, about 15 minutes. Season to taste with salt and pepper, then stir into the beans. Add the chorizo and continue cooking the beans, stirring occasionally, for 10–15 minutes. Adjust seasonings. Remove bay leaf. Serve garnished with scallions and cilantro, and with lime wedges.

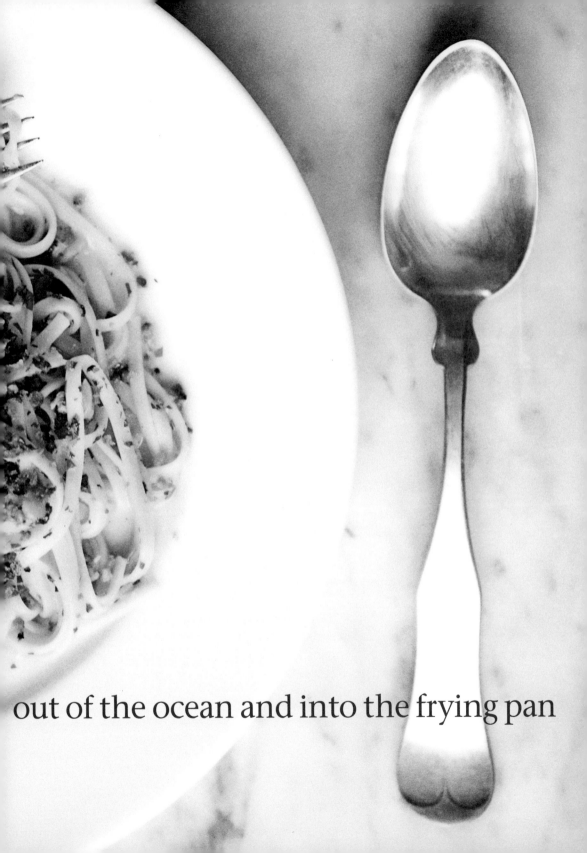

out of the ocean and into the frying pan

ANY NIGHT LINGUINE WITH CLAM SAUCE
serves 4–6

This is a real pantry meal, as we always have everything we need stashed in the cupboard—cans of delicate baby clams, bottles of clam broth, little jars of anchovies, and pasta. Cooking linguine in clam broth adds lots of flavor and pulls the whole dish together. We sprinkle toasted bread crumbs over the dish, Sicilian style, rather than grated cheese. We love the crunch that they add to the supple pasta.

FOR THE TOASTED BREAD CRUMBS
1 cup fresh bread crumbs
2–3 tablespoons olive oil
Salt

FOR LINGUINE WITH CLAM SAUCE
¼ cup olive oil
6 anchovy filets

2–4 cloves garlic, minced
Pinch of crushed red pepper flakes
½ cup white wine
32 ounces clam broth
Two 10-ounce cans baby clams
1 pound linguine
½ cup finely chopped fresh parsley

For the toasted bread crumbs, preheat the oven to 375° (or if you prefer you can sauté these in a skillet). Toss the bread crumbs with the olive oil and a pinch of salt in a bowl. Spread the bread crumbs out on a baking sheet and bake until dry and golden, about 10 minutes. Set aside to cool.

For linguine with clam sauce, heat the olive oil in a large deep skillet over medium-high heat. Add the anchovies and stir with a wooden spoon until they melt into the oil. Add the garlic and the red pepper flakes, and stir for a minute. Increase the heat to high, pour in the wine, clam broth, and the broth from the canned baby clams, cover, and cook until it comes to a boil. Add the linguine, and cook for about 10 minutes. Add the clams and their broth and continue to cook until the pasta has absorbed most of the broth. Add the parsley and toss everything together. Season to taste. Sprinkle each plate of pasta with the toasted bread crumbs.

Overleaf: Any Night Linguine with Clam Sauce

FRIED FISH
serves 4

Using fresh oil and maintaining a temperature of 360° will ensure that your fried fish will be tender, with a delicate crisp crust, and not the least bit greasy.

1½ pounds cod filet, cut into
  8 pieces the same size
1 cup milk
1 cup all-purpose flour
1 teaspoon baking powder

½ teaspoon salt
Canola oil
Tartar Sauce, (recipe below)
1 lemon, cut into wedges

Rinse the fish in cold water and pat dry with paper towel. Pour the milk into a shallow pan and add the fish, turning the pieces until they are drenched.

Sift the flour, baking powder, and salt together onto a platter. Dredge the pieces of fish in the flour, making sure to coat all sides.

Add enough oil to a medium pot to reach a depth of 2–3 inches. Heat the oil over medium heat until it is hot but not smoking (ideally to a temperature of 360°). Use a candy thermometer to check the temperature. As you fry, adjust the heat to maintain the temperature.

Working in batches, carefully slip the fish into the hot oil. Fry until golden brown, about 5 minutes, turning the fish over halfway through frying. Transfer fried fish with a slotted spatula to a wire rack set over paper towels to drain. Season with salt and serve hot with Tartar Sauce and wedges of lemon on the side.

TARTAR SAUCE

Why buy jarred tartar sauce when it's so simple to make? Everyone always has a jar of mayonnaise and a jar of capers knocking around in the door of their fridge. We prefer the sharp flavor of cornichons, but you could use another type of pickle or minced sweet onion or scallions, if you had to. Mix together ½ cup mayonnaise, 4–5 chopped cornichons, 1 tablespoon chopped capers with a splash of their pickling brine, and 4 finely chopped sprigs each of fresh parsley, dill, and tarragon in a small bowl. Stir in 1–2 tablespoons lemon juice and salt and pepper to taste. The sauce will keep up to 1 week in the refrigerator. —— *makes ¾ cup*

FISH STICKS
makes about 20

Some years ago, while on vacation in northern California with my family, we stopped in Sacramento to visit Corti Brothers (it is, after all, "the best grocery store in the world", page 7) and say hello to owner Darrell Corti. He insisted we join him for a quick lunch, so off to The Waterboy we went. We ordered fish sticks, drank wines that Darrell had brought along, and shared conversation I didn't even know I was capable of keeping up with. Our quick lunch lasted for hours. What we drank and all that we talked about is a little foggy to me now, but my family never forgot those real (and really good) fish sticks.

It turns out that we weren't the only ones crazy for chef-owner Rick Mahan's fish sticks. They'd started out nine years before as a staff meal favorite, and then turned into a popular menu item he still offers half a dozen times a year. Rick uses a local fish called rock cod, similar to Atlantic cod, but any good firm, flaky white fish will do. Goodbye, Mrs. Paul's. Hello, Mr. Mahan's! —— MH

1½ cups panko   1 pound cod filet, preferably center cut
1 cup flour   Salt and pepper
3 eggs   Canola oil

Pulse the panko in a food processor until the crumb is fairly fine, then transfer it to a wide dish. Put the flour in another wide dish. Beat the eggs in a third wide dish. Set aside.

Cut the fish into fat, evenly thick sticks about ¾ inch thick by 3 inches long. Season them all over with salt and pepper. Dredge the fish, one piece at a time, first in the flour, then in the eggs, then in the panko. If you like, set the fish sticks on a wire rack to rest as you bread them, up to an hour before frying them.

Add enough oil to a large cast-iron skillet to reach a depth of 1–2 inches. Heat the oil over medium heat until it is hot but not smoking, ideally to a temperature of 350° (use a candy thermometer to check the temperature).

Working in batches to avoid crowding the skillet, fry the fish sticks in the hot oil until golden brown all over, 5–6 minutes. Transfer the fish sticks with metal tongs or a slotted spatula to a wire rack set over paper towels to drain. Season with salt while still hot. Serve with lemon wedges and/or Tartar Sauce (page 73).

Left: above, Fish Sticks; below; Fried Fish (page 73)

CRAB CAKES
makes a dozen 2-inch cakes

These small piles of perfect jumbo lump crabmeat, with just the scantiest coating of batter holding them together, are the best Maryland crab cakes we've had. There are two secrets. The first is to mix all of the ingredients except the crab together, then fold the meat in ever so gently, and always by hand. The second is to use buttery Ritz crackers instead of bread crumbs. We like two-bite crab cakes—their smaller size makes them easier to cook.

2 tablespoons butter
3 ribs celery, minced
3 scallions, minced
1 egg
3 tablespoons mayonnaise
1 tablespoon fresh lemon juice
1 teaspoon Worcestershire sauce
½ teaspoon dry mustard

2 teaspoons Old Bay Seasoning
½ teaspoon salt
½ teaspoon pepper
8 Ritz crackers, crushed into coarse crumbs (⅓ cup)
1 16-ounce can jumbo lump crabmeat, drained
1 tablespoon vegetable oil

Melt 1 tablespoon of the butter in a skillet over medium-low heat. Add celery and scallions and cook until soft, 7–10 minutes. Remove from heat and let cool.

Whisk together the egg, mayonnaise, lemon juice, Worcestershire sauce, mustard, Old Bay Seasoning, salt, and pepper in a large bowl. Stir in the cracker crumbs and the cooled celery and scallions. Add the crabmeat and mix together very gently with your hand. Don't break up the crabmeat.

Make twelve 2-inch crab cakes, gently pressing each cake together in your hands, and arrange the cakes on a parchment-lined tray. It may seem like the crab cakes are in danger of falling apart, but chilling them will hold them together. Loosely cover the tray with plastic wrap and refrigerate for 1–2 hours.

To cook the crab cakes, heat the remaining 1 tablespoon of butter and the vegetable oil in a large nonstick skillet over medium to medium-low heat. Fry the cakes until golden brown on each side, 4–5 minutes. Serve with lemon wedges, Tartar Sauce (page 73), and saltine crackers, if you like.

hot chicks

CANAL HOUSE "ROTISSERIE" CHICKEN
serves 6

We lust after those golden spinning rotisserie chickens at our grocery store (what a great idea), but whenever we indulge, it's a tasteless, dry disappointment. If you've had the same experience, and like us, you don't have a rotisserie in your kitchen, go ahead and "spit-roast" your bird the way we do—directly on an oven rack in a hot oven. We slide a pan of vegetables on the rack below to catch and soak up the bird's drippings and juices.

1 chicken, 5–6 pounds
3–6 tablespoons good olive oil
Salt
1 small bunch fresh thyme
4–6 carrots, peeled and cut into
   large chunks

6–8 cloves garlic, peeled
3 russet potatoes, peeled and cut
   into large chunks
3 small yellow onions, halved
   or quartered
4 thick slices crusty bread, optional

Arrange one oven rack in the middle of the oven and another rack in the lower third of the oven. Preheat the oven to 400°. Rinse the chicken and pat it dry with paper towels. Rub it with 1–2 tablespoons olive oil then season it well with salt. Stuff the cavity with the thyme. Tuck the wing tips neatly behind the back of the chicken or snip them off. Set the chicken aside.

Put the carrots, garlic, potatoes, and onions into a large shallow roasting pan and rub with 2 tablespoons oil. Make a little room between the vegetables to accommodate the slices of bread, if using, tucking them in around the perimeter of the pan. Drizzle bread with 2 tablespoons oil. Season with salt.

Place the chicken in the oven breast side up directly on the upper rack in the middle of the oven. Put the pan of vegetables on the lower rack beneath the bird to catch the drippings. Roast the chicken and vegetables for 15 minutes, then pour 2 cups water into the pan. After about 30 minutes, tip any accumulated juices out of the chicken cavity into the pan below.

Continue roasting the chicken until the skin turns crisp and golden and the thigh juices run clear when pricked, 30–45 minutes. Lift the chicken off the rack and let it rest in the pan with the vegetables out of the oven for 10–15 minutes before carving. Serve the chicken, vegetables, and bread together.

GINGERED CHICKEN IN CREAM
serves 4–6

Serve this luxurious chicken with a fragrant rice like basmati or jasmine.

Kosher salt

1 tablespoon garam masala

2 tablespoons Ginger-Garlic Paste
(page 52)

1 chicken, 3–4 pounds, rinsed; dried

1 large yellow onion, thinly sliced

Extra-virgin olive oil

2 cinnamon sticks

1 cup heavy cream

1 small bunch cilantro, finely chopped

Rub 1 tablespoon salt, then the garam masala, then the Ginger-Garlic Paste
all over the chicken, inside and out. Truss the chicken with kitchen string. Put
it in a plastic bag and refrigerate for at least 4 hours and up to 2 days.

Preheat the oven to 450°. Put the onions in the bottom of a roasting pan.
Drizzle with a little olive oil. Add the cinnamon sticks and 2 cups water. Place
the chicken on the onions and roast until the bird is golden and the thigh
registers 155° on a meat thermometer, about 1 hour.

Remove the pan from the oven and transfer the chicken to a platter. Set
the roasting pan on the stovetop over medium heat and whisk in the heavy
cream. Cut the chicken into serving pieces. Strain the sauce (or not, just discard the cinnamon sticks) and pour over the chicken. Garnish with cilantro.

CHICKEN & RICE

This is a version of Atlanta chef Scott Peacock's family recipe and we both
love it. Melt 3 tablespoons butter in a large heavy skillet or pot over medium
heat. Add 1 cut-up chicken (2 wings tipped, 2 legs, 2 thighs, and a quartered breast) and cook, turning the pieces often, until they are just golden,
about 10 minutes. Add 1 finely chopped yellow onion and 3 finely chopped
celery ribs with their leaves, and season well with salt and pepper. Add 1 cup
water, cover, reduce heat to low, and cook for 20 minutes. Uncover, add 1
cup short- or long-grain rice, pushing the rice into the spaces around the
chicken. Increase heat to medium-low, add 1 cup water, cover, and cook until
the rice absorbs all the broth. Add more water if needed. — *serves 4–6*

Overleaf: Canal House "Rotisserie" Chicken

CHICKEN CORDON BLEU
serves 2

Our variation on this classic—we make a little pocket in the chicken breast and slip in the ham and cheese—will make any home cook a blue-ribbon winner.

2 thin slices boiled ham

2 thin slices melting cheese, such as Munster, Fontina, or Gruyère

½ cup flour

1 cup panko

1 egg

1 whole boneless, skinless chicken breast, cut in half to separate it into 2 lobes

Salt and pepper

Canola oil

Lay each slice of ham on a cutting board, put a slice of cheese on top of each, and fold the ham around the cheese as you would fold up a business letter. Set aside. Put the flour in a wide dish, put the panko in another, beat the egg in a third dish, and set them aside.

Lay each chicken breast half on the cutting board, smooth side facing down. If the breasts are big and fat, you can remove the tenderloin, if you like, and use it for another meal, but if the breasts are smaller and thinner, leave the tenderloins in place. They'll cover up any accidental nicks that may happen when cutting out the pocket in each breast. Using a narrow sharp knife with a pointed tip, make an incision in the side of the breast, then carefully cut out a long deep pocket without puncturing the rest of the breast. Repeat with the other breast. Tuck the ham and cheese into each pocket and gently press the breast to close up the pocket. Season the chicken with salt and pepper.

Add enough oil to a medium skillet to reach a depth of 1–2 inches. Heat the oil over medium heat until it is hot but not smoking, ideally to a temperature of 350° (use a candy thermometer to check the temperature).

Dredge one piece of chicken at a time in the flour, tapping off the excess, then dip it in the egg, then dredge it in the panko. Fry the chicken in the hot oil until golden brown all over and cooked through, about 5 minutes per side depending on the thickness of the breasts. Transfer the chicken to a wire rack set over paper towels to drain. Season with salt while still hot.

Right: above, Chicken Cordon Bleu; below, Chicken Kiev à la Canal House (page 84)

CHICKEN KIEV À LA CANAL HOUSE
serves 2

We omit the rolling and pounding scene from Gogol's *The Overcoat* when we make this delicious old-fashioned dish and simply slit pockets in each chicken breast, then tuck in the herb butter.

4 tablespoons softened butter
1 small handful combined fresh
  herb leaves, such as tarragon,
  parsley, chervil, and/or
  dill, chopped
Salt and pepper

1 whole boneless, skinless chicken
  breast, halved into 2 lobes
Canola oil
½ cup flour
1 egg, beaten
1 cup panko

Combine the butter, fresh herbs, and salt and pepper to taste in a small mixing bowl. Spread the butter out on a piece of plastic wrap or wax paper into a rectangle about 1 × 4 inches. Freeze the butter until hard, 20–30 minutes. (The cold butter won't melt as quickly when frying the chicken breasts.)

Lay each chicken breast half on a cutting board smooth side facing down. If the breasts are big and fat, you can remove the tenderloin, if you like, and use it for another meal, but if the breasts are smaller and thinner, leave the tenderloins in place. They'll cover up any accidental nicks that may happen when cutting out the pocket in each breast. Using a narrow sharp knife with a pointed tip, make an incision in the side of the breast, then carefully cut out a long deep pocket without puncturing the rest of the breast. Repeat with the other breast. Cut the cold herb butter in half crosswise, tuck one half into each pocket, and gently press the breast to close up the pocket. Season the chicken with salt and pepper. Keep the breasts cold in the refrigerator.

Add enough oil to a medium skillet to reach a depth of 1–2 inches. Heat the oil over medium heat until it is hot but not smoking (or until the temperature on a candy thermometer reaches 350°). Dredge one breast at a time in the flour, shaking off the excess, then dip it in the egg, and dredge in the panko. Fry until golden brown all over and cooked through, about 5 minutes per side depending on the thickness of the breasts. Transfer the chicken to a wire rack set over paper towels to drain. Season with salt while still hot.

ROASTED CHICKEN WINGS
serves 4

My mother is a great à la bonne femme cook, and I was fortunate to have been raised on her cooking—calves' brains in black butter, fragrant couscous, flaky bisteeya, whole sides of gravlax, boeuf à la bourguignonne and steak tartare, to name a few. But her simple roasted chicken wings are up there with the best.

She had a brood of seven to feed, and chicken wings were dirt cheap in the early seventies, priced to sell, mostly for making stock. Before spicy Buffalo chicken wings had migrated from upstate New York into American ubiquity, eating wings was a regular thing for us. She would buy them by the bagful, marinate them in a Lucite bowl as big as a birdbath, and roast them until they got crisp and brown and stuck to the pan. And that was our meal. A pile of meaty sticky wings, eaten with our fingers, always served with a leafy salad.

My mother doesn't cook elaborate dishes anymore, but her wings have prevailed. This past Christmas, having driven all day to get to her house in time for dinner, we sat down to a beautifully set table and ate chicken wings, with our fingers. ——MH

4 pounds (about 20) chicken wings, tips trimmed
Juice of 2 lemons
¼ cup extra-virgin olive oil
2 tablespoons Dijon mustard
2 teaspoons tarragon leaves, dried or fresh
Salt and pepper

Put the chicken wings, lemon juice, olive oil, mustard, tarragon, and salt and pepper to taste into a large bowl and rub the wings all over with the marinade. The wings can marinate at room temperature while the oven preheats, but if you want to marinate them longer (overnight is fine), cover the bowl with plastic wrap or transfer the wings to a resealable plastic bag and refrigerate them until later.

Preheat the oven to 375°. Spread the wings out on a roasting pan in a single layer, skin side up, drizzling any of the remaining marinade over them. Roast the wings until they are well browned and the skin papery crisp, about 1 hour. The pan juices and marinade will have caramelized and some of the wings will need to be pried off the pan. Eat wings hot or at room temperature with your fingers.

the meat of the matter

DELUXE DINNER OF BOILED MEATS
serves 12

Every country has its version of a boiled dinner with slowly simmered meats and a broth delicious enough to be the first course. Northern Italy has the elaborate *bollito misto*, with meats, fowl, and the fat pork sausage called *cotechino*, accompanied by *mostarda* (fruits preserved in sweet-spicy mustard syrup), and a piquant green sauce. France has *pot-au-feu*. Spain has the sumptuous *cocido* with boiled meats, vegetables, and chickpeas; the broth is served first, impregnated with *fideos* or thin egg noodles. At Canal House, we take a little from all of them and make our own version.

FOR THE BOILED MEATS
1 breast of veal, 4–5 pounds
2 large yellow onions, peeled
4 carrots, peeled
4 ribs celery
2 bay leaves
2–3 sprigs fresh thyme
10 black peppercorns
1 beef tongue, about 3 pounds
1 beef brisket, 3–5 pounds
1 chicken, 4–5 pounds, rinsed

Salt
4 russet potatoes

FOR THE GREEN SAUCE
1 bunch parsley, leaves chopped
10 cornichons, chopped
¼ cup cornichon pickling brine
¼ cup capers, coarsely chopped
½ cup extra-virgin olive oil

FOR THE FIRST COURSE
1 pound fideos or fine egg noodles

For the boiled meats, use a stockpot that is large enough to accommodate all the meats and aromatics and plenty of water to cover them. A large canning pot works well if your stockpot is too little. Or use a couple of large pots and split the veal breast and aromatics between them; simmer the brisket in one pot and the tongue and chicken in the other. Now, from the pots to the cooking. Put the breast of veal, onions, carrots, celery, bay leaves, thyme, and peppercorns into the pot and cover with cold water by 3 inches. Bring to a boil over high heat, skimming any foam that rises to the surface. Reduce the heat to medium.

Add the meats to the pot in stages, starting with the one that takes the longest to cook. The tongue goes in first (it takes 3½–5 hours), then the brisket (it needs 3–4 hours), and the chicken last (depending on its size and age—old birds take longer—so add it 1–2 hours before the other meats are finished).

Bring the broth back to a good simmer after each addition, skimming any foam that rises to the surface. Then reduce the heat to medium-low to maintain a gentle simmer. Add more water to the pot as necessary to keep everything well submerged. Simmer the meats until they are tender when pierced with a meat fork. The tongue won't be tender until it is possible to peel off the pebbly skin. Remove it from the pot after 3–4 hours to check, returning it to simmer longer if it needs more time. Once the tongue is ready, peel off the skin and trim away the gristle while it's still hot. Return the tongue to the pot. It can continue to simmer in the pot until the brisket and chicken are tender.

Carefully remove the tongue, brisket, and chicken from the pot and set them aside on a large platter. Strain the broth through a sieve into another pot, discarding the breast of veal (it's too dry and spent to serve) and the aromatics. Return the strained broth to its original pot and season it well with salt. Skim off any fat you don't want. Return the meats and chicken to the broth in the pot and keep them warm over low heat until ready to serve.

Meanwhile, peel the potatoes and cut them in half. Put them in a medium pot, cover with cold water, add a big pinch of salt, and bring to a boil over high heat. Reduce the heat to medium and cook until tender when pierced with a fork, 20–30 minutes. Drain the potatoes, reserving 2 cups of the cooking water. Pass the potatoes through a ricer into a bowl and thin them with 1½–2 cups of the reserved cooking water. Season with salt. Transfer them to a serving dish and cover them to keep warm.

For the green sauce, put the parsley, cornichons, their brine, and the capers into a bowl and stir in the olive oil. Set aside.

For the first course, bring 18–20 cups of the broth to a boil in another large pot over medium-high heat. Add the fideos and cook, stirring occasionally, until tender, 8–11 minutes. Serve the broth and noodles in warm soup bowls.

Carve the tongue, brisket, and chicken. Arrange them in a large, deep serving platter. Ladle some broth over all. Serve the meats, chicken, and broth at the table with the mashed potatoes. Pass the green sauce and extra salt and pepper at the table so your guests can season their boiled dinner as they like.

Overleaf: Deluxe Dinner of Boiled Meats

DAUBE
serves 6

Daube is usually made with red wine; our recipe uses Madeira and raisins to add an underlying mellow richness. Cold tart pickles create the perfect counterpoint.

1 cup flour
Salt and pepper
4 pounds quality beef chuck, cubed
4 tablespoons olive oil
1 cup Madeira or port
3 cloves garlic

Peel of ½ orange
Handful of raisins
2 large sprigs fresh rosemary
3 cups rich chicken broth (page 30)
2 pounds small boiling onions
Cold fresh dill pickles, chopped

Preheat the oven to 275°. Sift together the flour and salt and pepper to taste into a large bowl. Dredge the meat in the seasoned flour and shake off any excess. Heat 3 tablespoons of the oil in a large enameled cast-iron pot with a lid over medium-high heat. Working in batches, brown the meat on all sides in the hot oil, about 5 minutes per batch. Add more oil if needed. Transfer the browned meat to a large plate as you work.

Pour the Madeira into the pot, increase the heat to high, and stir with a wooden spoon, scraping up any browned bits stuck on the bottom of the pot. Cook until the Madeira has reduced by half, about 2 minutes. Reduce the heat to medium, add the garlic, orange peel, raisins, and rosemary, and cook for a couple of minutes. Add the chicken broth and cook until the broth is hot.

Return the meat to the pot, cover, and cook in the oven. While the meat cooks, blanch the onions in a pot of boiling water for about 2 minutes, then drain in a colander. When cool enough to handle, trim off root ends, then slip off papery skins. After the daube has cooked for about 2½ hours, add the onions to the pot. Cook until the meat and the onions are tender, about 1 hour.

Remove the pot from the oven and use a slotted spoon to lift out the meat and onions, taking care to keep the onions whole. Spoon off any fat, then strain the sauce through a fine sieve into a bowl, discard the solids, and return the sauce to the pot. If the sauce is thin, cook over medium-high heat until it reduces and thickens slightly. Return the meat and onions to the pot. Serve on mashed potatoes if you like, garnished with chopped pickles.

STUFFED CABBAGE
serves 8–12

It is well worth the time to make these cabbage packets. Each stuffed leaf is like a little gift.

FOR THE TOMATO SAUCE
6 cups strained tomatoes
1 pound lamb neck bones
1 medium onion, halved
1 cinnamon stick
Salt and pepper

FOR THE CABBAGE
1 large head savoy cabbage, cored

⅓ cup dried currants
2 tablespoons bourbon or Madeira
½ cup long-grain rice
2 tablespoons butter
1 medium onion, finely chopped
1 clove garlic, minced
1 pound ground lamb
½ teaspoon ground cinnamon
Salt and pepper

For the tomato sauce, put the tomatoes, 4 cups water, lamb neck bones, onions, cinnamon stick, and salt and pepper to taste in a medium pot and gently simmer over medium-low heat for about 1 hour. Adjust the seasonings.

For the cabbage, bring a large pot of water to a boil over high heat. Plunge the cabbage into the water, and blanch it until the outer leaves are tender, about 5 minutes. Transfer the head to a colander to drain. Carefully separate the tender leaves from the head. Return the cabbage to the boiling water and repeat the process until you have 14 large leaves. Set the leaves aside. Core and thinly slice the remaining interior of the cabbage and put it in a large enameled cast-iron or other heavy pot with a lid.

Soak the currants in the bourbon in a medium bowl to plump them. Put the rice into a small pot, cover with cold water by 2 inches, and gently boil over medium heat for 5 minutes. Drain; add the rice to the bowl with the currants.

Melt the butter in a medium skillet over medium heat. Add the onions and garlic, and cook, stirring often, until soft but not colored, 5–10 minutes. Add the onions and garlic to the bowl with the rice. Add the ground lamb, cinnamon, 1 tablespoon salt, and pepper to taste. Gently mix the filling together.

Lay 12 of the cabbage leaves out on a clean work surface. Put about ⅓ cup of

continued

93

continued

the filling in the center of each leaf. Working with one leaf at a time, fold over the sides, then gently roll the cabbage up to form a neatly filled package, more round than cylindrical. Repeat with the remaining leaves to make 12 stuffed cabbage leaves. Arrange the stuffed cabbage packets, seam side down, in the pot on top of the sliced cabbage, nestling them in one or two layers.

Discard the lamb neck, onions, and cinnamon stick from the tomato sauce and ladle it into the pot over the stuffed cabbages. Drape the remaining 2 cabbage leaves over the packets. Cover the pot with the lid. Bring to a simmer over medium-high heat. Reduce the heat to medium-low and simmer until the cabbage leaves are soft and supple, 2–3 hours.

DRUNKEN SAUERKRAUT WITH SMOKED PORK CHOPS
serves 8

In the Baltimore area, where our colleague Julie Sproesser's grandmother Bernece lives, sauerkraut is a holiday tradition. The recipe she follows is an adaptation of one from Julia Child that calls for juniper berries and vermouth or white wine. As juniper berries are sometimes hard for Bernece to find, she douses her "drunken" sauerkraut instead with enough gin and vermouth to make several martinis. As the sauerkraut bakes, the booze, butter, and bacon mellow it into unexpected tenderness. We serve it with smoked pork chops when it's cold outside. When the weather warms up, we make a pot of it and serve it with grilled sausages and wieners.

We prefer the bright flavor of fresh or raw (unpasteurized) sauerkraut. Look for it, refrigerated, in the meat or deli section of the grocery store.

4 pounds fresh sauerkraut

10–12 ounces slab bacon, cut into ¾-inch cubes

9 tablespoons salted butter

2 medium yellow onions, thinly sliced

8 sprigs fresh parsley

2 sprigs fresh thyme

2 bay leaves

12 black peppercorns

1 cup gin

⅔ cup dry vermouth or dry white wine

3–3½ cups chicken broth (page 30)

4 smoked pork chops, optional

4 links smoked pork sausage, optional

continued

continued

Preheat the oven to 325°. Drain the sauerkraut in a colander and rinse thoroughly. Working with one small handful at a time, squeeze out as much liquid as possible from the sauerkraut, then pull it apart to separate the strands. Set aside.

Cook the bacon in a large enameled cast-iron or other heavy ovenproof pot with a lid over medium-low heat until most of the fat is rendered, 10–15 minutes. Lift out the bacon with a slotted spoon and set aside. Pour off all but 3–4 tablespoons of the fat. Add 8 tablespoons of the butter (if using unsalted butter, add 1 teaspoon salt) to the pot and when melted add the onions. Cook until translucent, 3–5 minutes. Return the bacon to the pot, add the sauerkraut, and gently stir until it's evenly coated with the buttery fat.

Wrap the herbs and peppercorns in a piece of damp cheesecloth and tie the bundle closed with kitchen string. Bury the bundle in the sauerkraut. Add the gin, vermouth or wine, and 3 cups of the chicken broth to the pot. The liquid should just cover the sauerkraut.

Cut a piece of parchment paper into a circle the diameter of the pot's lid and grease both sides of it with the remaining 1 tablespoon butter. Lay the paper directly on the surface of the sauerkraut, then cover the pot with the lid. Transfer the pot to the oven and braise the sauerkraut for 3 hours. Check to make sure the sauerkraut is not drying out. Add a little more chicken broth if it is. Return the pot to the oven, covered, and braise for 1½ hours more. The sauerkraut should absorb all of the liquid by the time it is finished cooking.

If using the pork chops and sausages, remove and discard the herb bundle 30 minutes before the sauerkraut has finished cooking. Lay the meats on top of the sauerkraut. Cover with the parchment paper, then cover the pot and return it to the oven to finish braising.

CHOPPED STEAK MARCHAND DE VIN
serves 4–6

My little girls and I used to drive through the golden hills of West Marin to Point Reyes Station to dine at charming Chez Madeleine. Sadly, it's gone now. They served this fancy sauce with gorgeous steaks, but also with a chopped steak piled high with crispy fries which we used to wipe our plates clean. Past owners Kristi and Chuck Edwards shared their recipe with us. —— CH

FOR THE SAUCE
3 shallots, minced
1 cup red wine
2 cups store-bought veal demi-glace
1 teaspoon fresh thyme leaves
1 small bay leaf
3 tablespoons cold unsalted butter, cut into small pieces
2 tablespoons finely chopped parsley

Salt and pepper

FOR THE CHOPPED STEAK
2 pounds ground round
2 shallots, minced
2 tablespoons finely chopped parsley
1 teaspoon fresh thyme leaves
Salt and pepper
1 egg yolk

For the sauce, put the shallots and wine in a heavy medium pan and cook over medium heat until the wine has reduced to ¼ cup and the shallots have softened, about 10 minutes. Add the demi-glace, thyme, and bay leaf, and cook until the sauce just comes to a simmer. Reduce heat to low and cook until the sauce reduces by half and thickens, about 20 minutes. Remove bay leaf. Whisk in the butter, a piece at a time, until it is completely incorporated and the sauce is smooth with a lovely sheen. Stir in the parsley. Season with salt and pepper. Cover and set the pan in a larger one filled with hot water to keep the sauce warm.

For the chopped steak, put the meat, shallots, parsley, thyme, salt and pepper to taste, and egg yolk in a mixing bowl. Using two forks, mix together without compacting the meat. Form the meat into 4–6 oval patties. Use a knife to cross-hatch the surface of the patties on both sides. Heat a large heavy nonstick or cast-iron skillet over medium-high heat. Put the patties in the skillet and cook on both sides until brown, about 3 minutes per side for medium-rare. Spoon a little warm sauce onto a plate, place a patty on top of the sauce, then spoon more sauce over the top. Repeat with remaining patties. Serve with fries, if you like.

A
Celebration
of
Spring

STUFFED SPRING EGGS
makes 24 halves

Eggs can be impossible to peel if they are fresh. The cooked egg clings to the inside of the shell and the whites tear as you peel. Cooking older eggs seems to solve this problem, so we keep an extra dozen stashed in the fridge just for boiling. For variety, we also top our eggs with crispy bacon shards, anchovies, a little harissa, or a curl of smoked salmon.

Since we use only the asparagus tips for these eggs, we peel the rest of the spears, finely chop them, and add them to salads for a bit of green crunch.

Tips from 12 fresh asparagus
   spears, halved lengthwise
Really good extra-virgin olive oil
Salt and pepper
12 large eggs, at least 1 week old

½ cup mayonnaise
2 tablespoons sour cream
1 tablespoon Dijon mustard
Handful fresh chives, minced
Handful fresh chervil, chopped

Cook the asparagus tips in a small pot of boiling water over high heat until just tender, about 2 minutes. Drain, then dress the asparagus with olive oil and season with salt and pepper. Set aside.

Put the eggs in a single layer in a large pot. Add enough cold water to cover the eggs by 1 inch. Cover and bring to a boil over high heat. Remove from the heat and set aside for 18 minutes. Drain, then quickly cool the eggs in cold water (add a few ice cubes to help cool them down more quickly). Allow them to cool in the water for about 10 minutes. Tap the eggs on the kitchen counter, cracking the shells. Peel off the shells under cold running water.

Halve the cooled eggs lengthwise. Carefully remove the yolks from the whites. Put the yolks into a fine strainer and use a rubber spatula or big spoon to push them through the mesh into a bowl. (Or if you prefer, use a food processor.) Add the mayonnaise, sour cream, and mustard. Season to taste with salt and pepper. Add a little more mayonnaise if the yolks are too stiff. Fold in some of the chives and chervil.

Put the filling into the hollows of the whites, push an asparagus tip into the top of each egg, then drizzle with a drop or two of olive oil. Sprinkle with the remaining chives and chervil.

STEW OF BABY ARTICHOKES & FAVAS
serves 8–12

A "baby" artichoke, about the size of a jumbo egg, isn't immature—just small. It grows on the same plant as the big thistle does, but closer to the ground, shaded by the large saw-tooth leaves. It never develops a fuzzy interior choke, so with minimal preparation, the little darling can be eaten whole. You'll see baby artichokes at the grocery store off and on throughout the year, but spring is really their time.

24 baby artichokes

½ lemon

¾ cup extra-virgin olive oil

1 medium yellow onion, halved and thinly sliced

2 cloves garlic, thinly sliced

1 cup white wine

1 cup chicken broth (page 30)

Salt and pepper

One 28-ounce bag (6 cups) frozen fava beans

2 cups frozen baby sweet peas

½ bunch fresh mint, leaves chopped

½ bunch fresh parsley, leaves chopped

Pull off and discard the tough outer leaves of the artichokes until you get to the tender pale green inner leaves. Slice off about 1 inch from the top. Peel the stems, trimming off any dry or blemished ends. Squeeze the lemon into a bowl of cold water and add the artichokes as they are trimmed.

Put ½ cup of the olive oil, the onions, and garlic into a large heavy nonreactive pot (not aluminum or cast iron) and cook over medium heat until just soft, about 5 minutes. Drain the artichokes. Add them to the pot along with the wine and broth. Season with salt and pepper. Cover and stew the artichokes until they are very tender when pierced, 35–45 minutes.

While the artichokes are cooking, bring a pot of water to a boil. Blanch the favas for 1 minute. Drain, then cool under cold running water. Peel off and discard the tough outer skins. Put the tender bright green favas into a bowl.

When the artichokes are tender, scatter the favas and peas into the pot. Cover and simmer until warmed through, 5–10 minutes. Put the vegetables along with all their juices on a platter. Drizzle with the remaining ¼ cup olive oil, season with salt and pepper, and scatter the fresh herbs on top. Serve warm or at room temperature.

SAVORY ASPARAGUS BREAD PUDDING
serves 8

We use fat asparagus for this cheesy bread pudding, because the spears stay nice and plump. You can assemble this a day in advance. Keep it in the refrigerator overnight, then pop it into the oven to bake the next day.

1 loaf challah, sliced	6 eggs
3 ½ cups milk	Pepper
Salt	2 cups grated Gruyère
2 pounds fat asparagus, trimmed and peeled (page 40)	½ cup freshly grated parmigiano-reggiano
4 tablespoons butter	

Arrange the slices of challah in a single layer on a sheet pan. Save or discard the end pieces. Pour 2½ cups of the milk over the bread and set aside until the bread has absorbed the milk.

Bring a medium pot of salted water to a boil over high heat. Add the asparagus and boil until just tender, 2–3 minutes. Drain, then plunge the spears into a bowl of ice-cold water to stop them from cooking. Drain the asparagus, slice them in half lengthwise, and set aside.

Preheat the oven to 350°. Butter a large baking dish with 2 tablespoons of the butter. Beat the eggs with the remaining 1 cup of milk in a medium bowl. Season well with salt and pepper.

Line the bottom of the prepared baking dish with half the bread in a single layer. Cover the bread with half the asparagus. Scatter half the Gruyère then half the parmigiano-reggiano over the asparagus. Season with salt and pepper. Make another layer with the remaining slices of bread and the asparagus. Pour the beaten eggs and milk over the layers, scatter with the remaining cheeses, and dot the top with the remaining 2 tablespoons of butter.

Bake the bread pudding until puffed and golden brown, and set in the center, 45–60 minutes.

EASTER HAM
serves a crowd

A big handsome haunch of a ham befits a celebratory meal like Easter. We present it at the table, this sweet, apple-infused, golden crumb-encrusted ham, like a giant jewel. We like its tah-dah factor, but more important, a big bone-in ham, like this, has great flavor.

Figure three people per pound, great if you're having a good-size crowd. If your guest list is smaller, just send everyone home with leftovers.

One 16-pound bone-in
   smoked ham
2 gallons apple cider
¼ cup extra-virgin olive oil

3 cups fresh bread crumbs
1 cup dark brown sugar
¼ cup Dijon mustard

Put the ham fat side up into a large deep pot with a lid. Add enough cider just to cover the ham. Cover the pot and bring to a simmer over medium-high heat. Reduce the heat to medium-low and gently simmer the ham for 4 hours.

Heat the olive oil in a large skillet over medium heat until warm. Add the bread crumbs and toast them, stirring frequently, until golden, about 3 minutes. Set them aside. Put the brown sugar and mustard into a small bowl and stir until it becomes a thick paste. Set aside.

Preheat the oven to 400°. Carefully transfer the ham to a large roasting pan. Put about 1 cup of the cooking liquid in the bottom of the pan and discard the rest. Score the top of the ham with a sharp knife. Spread the sugar-mustard paste over the ham. Pack the bread crumbs on top. Bake the ham until the crumbs are browned and crisp and the juices in the bottom of the pan are sticky, about 30 minutes. Let the ham rest for at least 15 minutes before carving.

MERINGUES WITH STRAWBERRIES & ROASTED RHUBARB
makes 8

Meringues are simple to make, but need a little rest in the oven after they've baked. We like to make ours in the evening, when the kitchen is quiet, and let them cool in the turned-off oven overnight.

FOR THE MERINGUES
4 large egg whites, at room
    temperature
Pinch of cream of tartar
1 cup superfine sugar
1 teaspoon vanilla extract

FOR THE FRUIT
1 pound fresh rhubarb, thickly sliced

4–6 tablespoons sugar
¼ cup red wine
1 vanilla bean, split lengthwise
1 pint small ripe strawberries,
    hulled, and larger berries halved

1½ cups heavy cream

For the meringues, preheat the oven to 275°. Line a baking sheet with parchment paper; set aside. Beat egg whites and cream of tartar together in a large mixing bowl on medium speed until frothy. Increase speed to medium-high. Continue beating, gradually adding the sugar 1–2 tablespoons at a time. Increase speed to high and beat until whites are thick, glossy, and stiff, and the sugar has completely dissolved, 5–15 minutes. Rub some whites between your thumb and forefinger to feel if any granules remain. Beat in the vanilla.

Plop 8 equal spoonfuls of the meringue onto the parchment paper about 2 inches apart. Use the back of the spoon to make a shallow crater in the center of each. Bake for 1 hour. Turn off the oven and leave the meringues inside, undisturbed, to dry out and cool for at least 2 hours or overnight.

For the fruit, preheat the oven to 350°. Put the rhubarb into a heavy medium ovenproof pot. Add 4 tablespoons of the sugar, the wine, and vanilla bean. Roast the rhubarb until tender, about 30 minutes. Cool to room temperature. Meanwhile, toss the strawberries with the remaining 1–2 tablespoons sugar in a medium bowl and set aside until the berries release their juices, 1 hour.

Beat the heavy cream in a large bowl until soft peaks form. To serve, spoon some of the rhubarb and strawberries, along with their syrupy juices, on each meringue and top with a big dollop of the whipped cream.

SWEETIES

WINTER SUMMER PUDDING
serves 6

It's hard to imagine fruit frozen hard as marbles amounting to anything juicy or delicious. But raspberries and blackberries (don't bother with peaches or strawberries) do come to life, releasing their intense sweet-tart juiciness.

6 slices white sandwich bread, crusts removed

10–12 ounces (about 3 cups) frozen raspberries

10–12 ounces (about 3 cups) frozen blackberries

⅓ cup plus 2 tablespoons sugar

Heavy cream, optional

Preheat oven to 400°. Lay the bread out to dry a bit on the counter while the oven heats up. Toss the frozen berries with ⅓ cup of the sugar in a 10 × 14-inch baking dish. Slather the bread on one side with butter. Cut each slice in half diagonally. Buttered side up, arrange the triangles over the fruit so they overlap slightly, and sprinkle with the remaining 2 tablespoons sugar.

Bake until the fruit is bubbling and the bread is deep golden brown, about 45 minutes. Serve warm with a spoonful of heavy cream on top or with a scoop of vanilla ice cream, if you like.

ROASTED ORANGE MARMALADE TOAST
serves 4–6

We serve this as an afternoon sweet, adding a drizzle of heavy cream to each dish. For breakfast, we like to take the golden toasts right from the pan, scooping up the warm sticky marmalade on each.

3 slices white sandwich bread, crusts removed

2 navel oranges, washed under warm water to remove the waxy coating

2 cups fresh orange juice (8 oranges)

¾ cup demerara sugar

4–5 tablespoons butter (preferably salted), at room temperature

Preheat the oven to 325°. Lay the bread out to dry a bit on the counter while preparing the oranges. Trim off the stem and blossom ends of each orange. Halve the oranges lengthwise and thinly slice. Arrange them in a 9 × 12-inch baking dish so they overlap. Pour 1 cup of the orange juice over the oranges and sprinkle with ¼ cup of the sugar. Cover the dish with foil and roast the oranges until the peel and pith are soft and saturated with the thin juicy syrup, about 1½ hours.

Uncover the dish and sprinkle ¼ cup of sugar over the oranges. Increase the oven temperature to 375° and continue roasting, uncovered, until the oranges just begin to brown and the syrup thickens a little bit, 15–20 minutes.

Meanwhile, slather the bread on one side with butter. Cut each slice in half diagonally. Remove the dish from the oven and arrange the bread, buttered side up, on top of the fruit so they overlap. Sprinkle with 1 tablespoon sugar. Return to the oven and bake, uncovered, until the oranges and syrup are sticky and the bread is deep golden brown, 10–15 minutes.

Boil the remaining 1 cup orange juice and 3 tablespoons sugar together in a small heavy saucepan over medium-high heat, stirring often until syrupy, 5–10 minutes. Pour the syrup over the bread slices to moisten it. Serve warm.

APRICOT COMPOTE
makes about 4 cups

A spoonful of these apricots on their own or with a slice of Pound Cake (page 110) is a simple dessert to brighten a cold, wet, early spring day. Add a whole star anise to the pan with the other aromatics, or a drop or two of orange-flower water as the compote cools for a more fragrant syrup.

3 cups white wine
1½ cups sugar
Wide strips of zest from 1 lemon

1 vanilla bean, split lengthwise
1 cup dried apricots, halved crosswise

Put the wine, sugar, lemon zest, and vanilla bean in a medium saucepan over medium heat and gently boil, stirring often, until the sugar dissolves. Reduce the heat to medium-low and add the apricots. Cover and simmer until they are soft, about 10 minutes. Remove the pan from the heat and let the apricots cool in the syrup—they will plump up. The compote is better the following day and will keep in the refrigerator for up to 1 week. Discard the aromatics if storing the compote for more than one day.

Overleaf: left, Winter Summer Pudding; right, Roasted Orange Marmalade Toast

POUND CAKE
makes a great big cake!

This is the simplest cake in the world, made from an old recipe so basic you hardly need to write it down—a pound each of butter, sugar, eggs, and flour, all beaten together. Sounds easy, but it's how you beat it together that makes it really good. This large and serious cake has a beautiful dense crumb and can last up to a week. Eat it plain with a cup of tea, glazed with Lemon or Orange Syrup (below) or adorned with a fruit compote (like our Apricot Compote, page 109) and a plop of whipped cream. We toast thin slices for breakfast and spread them with a little butter—breakfast of champions.

1 pound unsalted butter, at room temperature
1 pound (2 cups) superfine sugar
1 pound (9 large) eggs
1 teaspoon vanilla extract
½ cup heavy cream
1 pound (3 cups) pastry flour
1 teaspoon salt
½ teaspoon cream of tartar
¼ teaspoon ground cardamom

Preheat the oven to 325°. Put the butter in the bowl of a standing mixer fitted with a whisk attachment and beat on high speed until light and fluffy, 8 minutes. Gradually add the sugar to the butter as you continue to beat, until the batter is creamy, about 5 minutes. Add the eggs one at a time, incorporating each completely before adding the next. Add the vanilla and heavy cream.

Sift together the flour, salt, cream of tartar, and cardamom into a bowl using a fine strainer. With the mixer on low speed, slowly add the sifted dry ingredients while you continue to beat the batter until it is all mixed together. At this stage don't overbeat the batter.

Pour the batter into a lightly greased nonstick angel food cake or tube pan. Bake until the top is golden and slightly split and a skewer poked into the center comes out clean, about 1 hour and 15 minutes.

LEMON OR ORANGE SYRUP ❦ Heat ½ cup fresh orange or lemon juice and ½ cup superfine sugar together in a small pan over medium heat, stirring with a wooden spoon until the sugar dissolves completely and the syrup thickens slightly. Remove from heat and allow to cool for a few minutes. Use a thin skewer and poke holes all over the top of the cake and brush it with the syrup.

APPLES TATIN
serves 4–8

This is a homey version of the French classic *tarte Tatin*. We use sweet, juicy Braeburn apples which hold their shape when they're cooked.

FOR THE PASTRY
1 cup pastry flour
6 tablespoons butter, cut into small pieces
1 egg

FOR THE APPLES
¾ cup sugar
4 tablespoons butter, cut into small pieces
6–7 apples, such as Braeburn, peeled and thickly sliced

For the pastry, put the flour into a mixing bowl. Cut the butter into the flour with a pastry blender until it resembles very coarse cornmeal. Crack the egg into a measuring cup, add enough water to equal ½ cup, and beat to mix together. Drizzle 4 tablespoons of the beaten egg into the dough, tablespoon by tablespoon, mixing it lightly with your hands. Reserve the remaining beaten egg. Press the dough into a flat disc, cover it with plastic wrap, and chill it in the refrigerator for about 1 hour.

For the apples, pour the sugar into a 9–10-inch ovenproof nonstick skillet. Scatter the butter pieces evenly on top, and over medium-high heat allow the butter and sugar to melt together without stirring. Tip the skillet from side to side to help them melt evenly. Carefully arrange the apples in several layers (don't burn your fingers) on top of the sugar, overlapping the slices.

Preheat oven to 375°. Cook the apples in the sugar without stirring or disturbing them except to press them down to help release their juices. Cook until the sugar turns golden brown and the juices are bubbling and have thickened slightly, about 30 minutes.

Roll the chilled dough out on a floured surface to form a 12-inch round. Roll the pastry around the rolling pin and unfurl it over the apples in the skillet, tucking in the edges. Brush with the reserved egg mixture and bake for 25 minutes. Allow to cool for 15 minutes, then loosen the edges with a knife. Place a flat platter on top of the skillet and carefully invert it to unmold the tart onto the platter. Don't burn yourself!

BOSTON CREAM PIE
makes 2 "pies"

This pie is actually a delicate cake and should be served "with plenty of good hot coffee", according to Alan Hooker, from whose recipe in *California Herb Cookery* (Edwin House Publishing, 1996) we adapted this one.

FOR THE CAKE
5 large eggs, at room temperature
1 cup sugar
1 cup cake flour, plus more for the pan
¼ cup pastry flour
1 teaspoon salt
¼ teaspoon nutmeg
2 tablespoons milk
½ teaspoon vanilla extract

FOR THE CUSTARD
2½ cups milk

½ cup sugar
4 tablespoons cornstarch
2 egg yolks
⅛ teaspoon salt
1 teaspoon vanilla extract
1 tablespoon Grand Marnier, optional
1 tablespoon unsalted butter

FOR THE CHOCOLATE ICING
1 cup chocolate chips
½ cup heavy cream

For the cake, preheat oven to 400°. Put the eggs and sugar in the bowl of a standing mixer fitted with a whisk, and beat for 15 minutes. (Be patient; this long beating is what makes this cake so light and delicate.)

Sift together the cake flour, pastry flour, salt, and nutmeg. Gradually add the dry ingredients to the beaten eggs while continuing to whisk. Add the milk and vanilla.

Grease two 8½-inch round cake pans and dust them with flour, tapping out any excess. Divide the batter between the 2 pans and bake until the tops are golden and a skewer poked into the center of the cakes comes out clean, 17–20 minutes. Unmold the cakes onto wax paper or parchment paper that has been sprinkled with sugar.

For the custard, heat 1½ cups of the milk and the sugar in a heavy saucepan over low heat, stirring until the sugar dissolves. Whisk together the remaining 1 cup milk, cornstarch, egg yolks, salt, vanilla, and Grand Marnier, if using. Gradually add it to the hot milk, stirring with a wooden spoon until the custard is thick and smooth, about 20 minutes. Keep heat low and stir from the bottom of the pan so the custard doesn't scorch. Stir in the butter then set aside to cool.

For the chocolate icing, heat the chocolate and cream in a small heavy pan over low heat, stirring until melted and smooth (or heat for about 1 minute in the microwave, then stir the cream and chocolate together).

To assemble, split each cake into 2 layers, spread the bottom layers with cooled custard, put on the top layers, and spread chocolate icing evenly over the tops.

BROWNIES
makes 2 dozen

Heating the butter and sugar together gives these brownies their distinctive taste and look—rich and fudgy, with a shiny, tissue paper-thin top crust.

14 tablespoons butter

1 cup flour, plus more for the pan

2 cups sugar

4 ounces semisweet chocolate, chopped

2 ounces unsweetened chocolate, chopped

1 teaspoon instant espresso powder, optional

¼ teaspoon salt

4 eggs

2 teaspoons vanilla extract

1 cup walnuts, chopped, optional

Preheat the oven to 350°. Grease a 9-inch square baking pan with 2 table-spoons of the butter, then dust it with flour, tapping out any excess.

Melt the remaining 12 tablespoons butter in a medium saucepan over medium heat. Add the sugar, stirring until it has the consistency of very soft slush and just begins to bubble around the edge of the pan, 1–2 minutes. Remove the pan from the heat. Add the chocolates, espresso powder, if using, and salt, stirring until the chocolate melts completely.

Put the eggs in a medium mixing bowl and beat them at medium speed with an electric mixer. Gradually add the warm chocolate mixture, about a quarter cup at a time, beating constantly until smooth. Stir in the vanilla. Add the flour and wal-nuts, if using, stirring until just combined. Pour the batter into the prepared pan.

Bake until a toothpick inserted into the center comes out clean, 45–60 minutes. Put the pan on a rack to cool. To serve, cut the brownies into 2-inch squares.

Overleaf: Boston Cream Pie

LITTLE CHOCOLATE TURNOVERS
makes about 16

We keep sheets of store-bought puff pastry in our freezer. The pastry defrosts as quickly as it takes to heat up the oven, so a batch of cheese straws or a savory or sweet tart can be put together quite spontaneously. These dainty chocolate turnovers were once a last-minute solution when dessert had been an afterthought. Serve them after dinner or, if something sweet is your thing in the morning, for breakfast.

Be sure the puff pastry you buy is made with butter. The ones made with vegetable shortening taste like flaky cardboard.

2 sheets frozen puff pastry, defrosted	½ cup heavy cream
Flour	3–4 tablespoons granulated sugar
One thin 4-ounce bar good chocolate, broken into 16 triangles, or 1 cup chocolate chips	Powdered sugar

Preheat the oven to 400°. Line a baking sheet with a piece of parchment paper and set aside.

Lay the puff pastry on a lightly floured work surface and dust the top with a little flour. Cut the pastry into sixteen 2½–3-inch squares. For each turnover, lay a piece of chocolate just inside one of the corners or quadrants of the pastry square (or fill a quadrant with about 1 tablespoon of the chocolate chips). Brush the edge of the pastry with some of the heavy cream. Fold the pastry in half over the chocolate, forming a nice little triangle or turnover. Crimp the edges together. Repeat with the remaining pastry squares and chocolate, making 16 turnovers in all. Arrange the turnovers on the prepared baking sheet at least 1 inch apart. (The turnovers can be frozen at this point and baked later, if you like. Once they are frozen solid, transfer them to a resealable plastic bag. They'll keep, frozen, for up to 1 month. They do not need to be defrosted before continuing with the recipe.)

Brush the turnovers with some heavy cream and sprinkle each with some of the granulated sugar. Bake until puffed and golden, about 10 minutes. Cool slightly before dusting with powdered sugar. Serve warm.

Breakfast All Day Long

NEEN'S BUTTERMILK LOVE CAKES
makes about 18 4-inch love cakes

Even as a child I knew my grandmother's hotcakes were special. I loved them, and I loved to help her in the kitchen. My first job was to separate the eggs for her. I'd tap one on the side of the bowl, cracking it in half. Catching the yolk in the cracked shells, I'd slip it back and forth while the gooey whites dripped down into the mixing bowl. Turning the red handle of her Cadillac of an eggbeater, with the smooth gears whirring, I'd whip up the whites into thick, billowy mounds. While she carefully measured the flour, the butter melted in an egg-poaching cup floating in a little pot of simmering water. The ritual never varied. Finally, she would start heating the griddle (purportedly made of "airplane aluminum", which gave it quite a provenance). She would test the griddle by flicking water on it, and when little beads danced across the hot metal, it was time to begin. Standing at her post at the stove, she flipped batch after batch until our big hungry family was fed. Flapjacks, hotcakes, pancakes—these were love cakes. ——CH

2 large eggs, separated
1 cup buttermilk
2 tablespoons melted butter
1 cup cake flour
1 tablespoon sugar

½ teaspoon baking powder
½ teaspoon baking soda
¼ teaspoon salt
Vegetable oil

Whisk the egg yolks into the buttermilk in a medium mixing bowl. Whisk in the butter. Put the flour, sugar, baking powder, baking soda, and salt into a sieve and sift it into the buttermilk. Lightly whisk until the batter is just mixed (a few lumps won't hurt).

Put the egg whites in a clean mixing bowl and beat with a whisk until soft peaks form. Use a rubber spatula to fold them into the batter. Don't overwork the batter, keep it light and fluffy.

Pour a little oil onto a nonstick griddle or large skillet. Wipe out the oil with a paper towel, leaving only the thinnest film. Heat the griddle over medium-high heat until hot. Pour about ¼ cup of batter on the griddle. Cook until little holes appear on the surface and the cooked side of the pancake—lift the edge to check—is golden brown, about 1 minute on each side. Slather on the butter and a few good glugs of real maple syrup.

SOUR CREAM PANCAKES
makes about 16 4-inch pancakes

When the angels took my grandmother, I thought her buttermilk pancake recipe had gone with her. So for years I used this recipe to approximate hers. I always have sour cream in the fridge and can easily whip up a batch for breakfast or supper. Sometimes I make tiny pancakes and instead of butter and maple syrup, I top them with a spoonful of trout roe—poor man's caviar.

Recently, my sister-in-law Mina e-mailed me the lost recipe, not quite the little index card with my grandmother's spidery old lady handwriting, but a treasure to me nonetheless. Now I am all stacked up with delicious pancakes. ——CH

1 cup sour cream
3 large eggs, separated
2 tablespoons melted butter
7 tablespoons cake flour

1 tablespoon sugar
½ teaspoon baking soda
½ teaspoon salt
Vegetable oil

Whisk the sour cream and egg yolks together in a medium mixing bowl. Whisk in the melted butter. Put the flour, sugar, baking soda, and salt into a sieve and sift it into the sour cream mixture. Lightly whisk until just mixed (a few lumps won't hurt anything).

Put the egg whites into a clean mixing bowl and beat with a whisk until soft peaks form. Use a rubber spatula to fold them into the batter. Don't overwork the batter, keep it light and fluffy.

Pour a little oil on a nonstick griddle or large skillet. Wipe out the oil with a paper towel, leaving only the thinnest film. Heat the griddle over medium-high heat until hot. Pour about ¼ cup of batter on the griddle. Cook until little holes appear on the surface and the cooked side of the pancake—lift the edge to check—is golden brown, about 1 minute on each side. Slather on the butter and a few good glugs of real maple syrup.

THE BEST WAFFLES IN THE WORLD
makes 16

It sometimes happens that you find a recipe that stops you in your tracks, one so perfectly delicious it becomes the standard bearer and eliminates forever the need to search further. For us, this waffle recipe, adapted from *The Fannie Farmer Cookbook* (Alfred A. Knopf, 1996), which was edited and largely rewritten by Marion Cunningham, is just such a one. Delicately yeasty and tender with a lacy crispness, these waffles are heaven on a plate.

One year I asked for a waffle iron for Christmas. I wanted to make this recipe for breakfast after we finished opening gifts. My husband bought the biggest waffle iron money could buy, wrapped it beautifully, and placed it under the tree. Following Marion's advice, I knew the iron that works with her recipe had to be a simple conventional one, not a Belgian waffle iron with crevices too deep for the delicate batter. So I secretly, carefully, unwrapped the gift before Christmas. My suspicions proved right. I exchanged the wrong waffle iron for the right one, rewrapped it, and back under the tree it went. On Christmas morning I opened my gift, kissed my husband, and we had waffles for breakfast. —— MH

Two 7-gram packages active dry yeast	2 teaspoons sugar
4 cups warm milk	4 cups all-purpose flour
16 tablespoons butter, melted	4 eggs
2 teaspoons salt	½ teaspoon baking soda

Dissolve yeast in 1 cup warm water in a large bowl; let rest for 5 minutes. Add the milk, butter, salt, sugar, and flour and beat until smooth. Transfer half of the batter to another large bowl (batter will double in volume). Cover both bowls with plastic wrap. Let batter stand overnight at room temperature.

The following day, beat 2 eggs and ¼ teaspoon baking soda into the batter in each bowl until well mixed (batter will be very thin). Pour ½ cup batter on a very hot waffle iron and let it set for 30 seconds, then lower the lid and cook until the waffle is golden brown and crisp, about 5 minutes. Repeat the process with the remaining batter. Serve with maple syrup and butter, if you like. The batter will keep for up to 2 days in the refrigerator.

CREAMED CHICKEN
serves 4

Although waffles are usually and rightly served anointed with butter and maple syrup, they are also delicious topped with something savory for a homey supper. We pick up a roast chicken at the store if we don't have time to cook our own.

4 tablespoons butter
3 tablespoons flour
Salt and pepper
Pinch of ground cayenne
Grated zest of 1 lemon

1 cup hot, chicken broth (page 30)
1½ cups hot whole milk
One 10-ounce package frozen peas
3 cups torn roast chicken pieces
½ cup chopped fresh chives

Melt the butter in a heavy medium pan over medium-low heat. Stir in the flour with a wooden spoon until it forms a smooth roux. Season with salt and pepper and cayenne. Add the lemon zest. Cook, stirring often, for about 3 minutes. Slowly add the chicken broth to the roux, stirring constantly. Gradually add the milk, stirring until the sauce is thick and smooth, about 15 minutes. Add the peas and chicken to the sauce, cover, and cook until it is hot, about 10 minutes. Taste and adjust the seasonings. Serve over hot waffles or white rice, garnished with lots of chopped chives.

EGGS À LA GOLDENROD

Melt 3 tablespoons butter in a heavy medium pan over medium-low heat. Stir in 3 tablespoons flour with a wooden spoon until it forms a smooth roux. Season with salt and pepper and 1 or 2 pinches each of ground cayenne and garam masala. Cook, stirring often, for about 3 minutes. Gradually add 1 cup hot, rich chicken broth (page 30) to the roux, stirring constantly. Gradually add 1 cup hot milk to the sauce, stirring constantly, until the sauce is thick and smooth, about 15 minutes. Add thickly sliced whites of 8 hard-boiled eggs to the sauce. Taste and adjust seasonings. Press the 8 cooked yolks through a sieve into a bowl. Serve the sauce over hot waffles, garnished with the egg yolks and lots of chopped chives. —— *serves 4*

OUR BOOKS

This is the sixth book of our recipe collections—Canal House Cooking. We publish three seasonal volumes a year, each filled with delicious recipes for you from us. To sign up for a subscription or to buy books, visit thecanalhouse.com.

OUR WEBSITE

Our website, thecanalhouse.com, a companion to this book, offers our readers ways to get the best from supermarkets (what and how to buy, how to store it, cook it, and serve it). We'll tell you why a certain cut of meat works for a particular recipe; which boxes, cans, bottles, or tins are worthwhile; which apples are best for baking; and what to look for when buying olive oil, salt, or butter. We'll also suggest what's worth seeking out from specialty stores or mail-order sources and why. And wait, there's more. We share our stories, the wines we are drinking, gardening tips, and events; and our favorite books, cooks, and restaurants are on our site—take a look.